THE PRACTITIONER INQ~~~~

Marilyn Cochran-Smith and Susan L. Lytle, Series Editors

Advisory Board: JoBeth Allen, Judy Buchanan, Curt Dudley-Marling, Robert Fecho,
Sarah Freedman, Dixie Goswami, Joyce E. King, Sarah Michaels, Luis Moll,
Susan Noffke, Sharon Ravitch, Marty Rutherford, Lynne Strieb, Diane Waff, Ken Zeichner

(continued)

AUTOBIOGRAPHY ON THE SPECTRUM

DISRUPTING THE AUTISM NARRATIVE

BETH A. MYERS

TEACHERS COLLEGE PRESS

TEACHERS COLLEGE | COLUMBIA UNIVERSITY

NEW YORK AND LONDON

Published by Teachers College Press, 1234 Amsterdam Avenue, New York, NY 10027

Copyright © 2019 by Teachers College, Columbia University

Cover design by adam b. bohannon

All rights reserved. No part of this publication may be reproduced or transmitted in any form or by any means, electronic or mechanical, including photocopy, or any information storage and retrieval system, without permission from the publisher. For reprint permission and other subsidiary rights requests, please contact Teachers College Press, Rights Dept.: tcpressrights@tc.columbia.edu

Library of Congress Cataloging-in-Publication Data is available at loc.gov

ISBN 978-0-8077-6145-8 (paper)
ISBN 978-0-8077-7782-4 (ebook)

Printed on acid-free paper
Manufactured in the United States of America

26 25 24 23 22 21 20 19   8 7 6 5 4 3 2 1

Contents

Acknowledgments

The crafting of this work was a journey that I could not have completed without the incredible support of so many in my life. My mentor, Susan Lytle, consistently reminded me that this work is important and pushed me to consider my teaching spaces as locations of inquiry. I wish to thank Elizabeth Cantafio and my brilliant and committed colleagues who engaged with me in this work, especially Rob Simon, Maria Ghiso, Gillian Maimon, and later Gerald Campano. I offer heartfelt thanks to Judith Vietri, my first principal and mentor, and those who worked tirelessly in our class, especially Kathleen McGee, Maria Ianarelli, and Pat Dolan. I would like to thank those at the Center as well as my colleagues at Syracuse University for giving me the opportunity to do the work I love in such supportive places. To the many scholars who engaged in this work before me, thank you for building a base from which we can climb.

Thank you to Sarah Biondello at TC Press for advocating for this work for so long and guiding this writing to publication, and to all those who provided invaluable feedback along the way. Thank you to both Susan Lytle and Marilyn Cochran-Smith for opening opportunities for this kind of work in their series.

Finally, I want to thank my family, especially my parents for their unwavering commitment to education; my children, Molly, Ella, Bobby, and Caroline, who always share space in my life with my students; and my husband, Rob Myers, who has taken many of the steps of this journey with me. I am grateful to him for seeing my potential even when I could not, for being confident in my work even when I was not, and for pushing me and lifting me up at the same time.

This work is dedicated to my students; I wish I could put all of their names here without compromising their anonymity, because they each deserve personal accolades for their contributions. They are brilliant makers.

Preface

Autobiography on the Spectrum: Disrupting the Autism Narrative offers
a critically unconventional perspective on autism—the view from adolescence. In the large scope of research on autism, little is written from the
position of individuals with autism themselves, and scant literature exists
that includes the voices of adolescents with autism. In fact, a considerable
amount of research disregards the ability of an autistic individual to describe
his or her own experiences and create personal accounts. The predominant
deficit model of autism positions it as a disorder that limits a person's ability
to understand and relate to others (Biklen, 2005; Smith, 1996). Other research claims that the emotional experiences of children with autism are so
limited that they cannot form narratives (Losh & Capps, 2006), relegating
those with autism to "unautobiographical lives" (Smith, 1996). These assumptions about autism can be very damaging to the experience of autistic
individuals, as teachers, clinicians, and even family and peers who are ex-
posed to these assumptions can view students with autism through this lens
of limitation. When autistic students are assumed to be unable to voice their
own opinions and relate their experiences, they are excluded from critical
learning points in schools and their communities. This cycle of limitation
can continue ad infinitum.

This book argues that adolescents with autism are not being represented in the current research, not because they are *unable* to represent their
own experiences, but because their experiences are not always valued. In
this work with children and adolescents, the students (and their creations)
contradict prevailing notions about autism. *Autobiography on the Spectrum*
elucidates how deficit constructions can marginalize individuals both in and
out of school. Through the lens of a *presumption of competence* (Biklen,
2005) and taking a critical inquiry stance, this book explores how children
and adolescents with autism can (and do) represent themselves to the world.

Autobiography on the Spectrum focuses on an in-depth analysis of a
yearlong inquiry group. The group, made up of 12 autistic adolescents and
one teacher, collaborated weekly to create multimedia autobiographical
projects. Through video production, photography, writing, drawing, speak-
ing, and other modes of expression, the youth explored their life experiences
and crafted works that demonstrated their understandings of themselves

and others. These projects addressed themes such as home and family, school and education, and the representation of disability. In this group, all of the teens took up questions about their identities as students with autism. This work shows the youth asserting ownership of their experiences and designing themselves as brokers of their own histories. Counter to the most prominent characterizations of autism (such as those from Autism Speaks, the Autism Science Foundation, the Association for Science in Autism Treatment, and many others), these students powerfully demonstrated their autobiographical lives.

This book is a purposeful work of practitioner inquiry. One of the strengths of practitioner inquiry is that it is multifaceted; that is, it creates spaces for the many perspectives and frameworks it can encompass (Cochran-Smith & Lytle, 2009). This multiplicity of perspectives is much needed to counter traditional disability models (see above). The emphasis on accountability that Cochran-Smith and Lytle (2009) point to as "toxic" to the practitioner research movement is especially present in the field of special education. When I was teaching as an inclusive elementary educator, many goals needed to be addressed on a daily and weekly basis. Quantitative data collection had to occur regularly and in a prescribed manner, and progress on each goal had to be reported with hard numbers (for example, "correct in 8 out of 10 trials for at least 3 consecutive days" or "demonstrates skill in 75% of observed instances during a school week"). This could have easily consumed my entire practice as a teacher, and our classroom staff had to make a concerted daily effort to foreground the children, the teaching, and the collective learning experience over the daily drilling and data collection. This was hard work then and is particularly hard work now that large-scale standardization has moved to such a prominent place in school reform; this kind of practitioner inquiry is complicated work about children and teaching that is enveloped in a system that has become about numbers. Cochran-Smith and Lytle (2009) point out just how disconnected this accountability model is from the real work of education:

> Yet even as teaching becomes more and more public, it remains, at its heart, radically local—embedded in the immediate relationship of students and teachers, shaped by the cultures of schools and communities, and connected to the experiences and biographies of individuals and groups. (p. 10)

Practitioner inquiry is a means of honoring students and their knowledge in a way that cannot extract the student, the teacher, or the pedagogy from the local. This book pushes against the much-examined test scores to paint a different picture of student knowledge.

I begin this work from the overarching stance that Biklen (2005) calls the *presumption of competence*. The dominant view of autism as deficit presumes that only the highest-functioning people with autism are able to hold views of themselves in relation to others. Biklen (2005), on the other hand, describes the presumption of competence as the premise that "people classified as autistic, even those who cannot speak, are thinking people with ideas about their lives and their relationship to the world" (p. 1). Presuming competence centers the focus on autistic individuals as people with abilities and strengths rather than as deviations from some mythical norm. Of particular importance in this work, the presumption of competence assumes that all individuals are knowers of their own lives.

Contrary to the view of autism as a medical condition to be treated or managed, this work allows for the multiple subjectivities that underlie the characterization of autism. I write this under the assumption that autism cannot be objectified and defined in a concrete way. This work is not meant to represent *all* people labeled with autism; nor is it meant to represent autism as separate from or internal to the individual. Rather, autism is seen as a social and cultural construct with multiple and subjective truths and identities. This book is meant to address the idea that definitions and models miss, as Carini (2001) explains, "the point of human differences and human complexity" (p. 9).

Carini (2001) challenges the notion of "normalcy and the consequent classifying and pathologizing of children" (p. 1). Her work at the Prospect School viewing children as "makers" has been an inspiration to this work. An aim of this study is to open the dialogue about students identified as autistic to the students themselves. One assumption of this work is that the students have unique perspectives on their own lives. Under this framework, they are not objects to be classified, medicalized, marginalized, or devalued, but individuals who can and do contribute to the knowledge of and dialogue about students, learning, and identity.

Autobiography on the Spectrum begins with an introduction to autism narrative and its place in the larger context of disability in society. Chapter 1 provides the necessary background to the inquiry, reviews a working definition of autism and problematizes that definition, introduces the reader to the notion that much of the current research on autism is from a deficit or medical model, and describes the setting for the project—a yearlong inquiry group in which teens created representations of their lived experiences and shared them with one another.

In the youth's work in the Teen Project, one of the recurrent topics that emerged was home and family. Chapter 2 details how the teens explored this topic in their representations, looking closely at the works of one teen and juxtaposing that work with examples from the rest of the group.

Chapter 3 examines the theme of education in the students' work. Despite this study taking place in an out-of-school setting, the topic of school permeated the teens' representations of their lives. Chapter 3 shows the ways in which the teens explored the theme of school and how they used their collective works to make sense of their school experiences. This chapter highlights three students and the stories they created in our inquiry group.

Chapter 4 focuses on the term *autism* as the youth understand and examine it, looking at the works of several members of the group as they wrestle with the words *normal* and *different*. Although autism itself often took a backseat in the stories the teens told, many of their works showed underlying themes of life with a label. These works demonstrated how much the medical model misses in defining these students.

The final chapter discusses the overarching issues that this work addresses. I offer a discussion of the themes and their significance in a world that relies on labeling, deliver a critique of the current state of autism research in light of these findings, and discuss implications and future research.

Autobiography on the Spectrum describes how space can be made for all adolescents to build their own representations of their lives. It is a warning against the use of labels to limit what students can do. The work of self-representation throughout this book is valuable to students, to teachers, and to the world. This work disputes the perception that people with autism are incapable of self-reflection and self-representation. The dominant discourse of education policy and the research community persists in portraying autism as a problem to be fixed. In contrast, this work demonstrates that these students, when given opportunities and support, display capabilities that often go unnoticed.

This book offers the possibility of creating a space for the voices of children and adolescents with autism to question the stereotypes of individuals considered "neurologically disabled." This work has been a recursive process, in which I have found more questions as the research developed and evolved. It is this work that I hope will challenge the social and political constructs of autism and contribute to the growing literature of education and critical disability theory as it relates to autism.

A FEW NOTES ABOUT THE TEXT

Throughout this book, I borrow from Riessman's (1993) definition of *personal narrative* as "talk organized around consequential events" (p. 3). I expand that definition to include other forms of communication and creation by using the term *narrative works*; I am considering *works* as Carini (2001) imagines the term, intertwined with and interdependent on all the acts that make a life. Additionally, I would include the idea that personal narratives are autobiographical. In personal narratives, individuals craft stories about particular events in their lives. Often, these stories highlight an event that has special consequence, such as when "there has been a breach between ideal and real, self and society" (Riessman, 1993, p. 3). Throughout this work, I use the terms *narrative* and *story* interchangeably.

There is great debate in the disability field over the use of person-first or identity-first language. The Deaf community, for example, has long identified with claiming the disability label as their own. Individuals labeled with intellectual disability, however, are often strong advocates for person-first language. When the work in this text first began, person-first language regarding autism was considered to be the preferred default. In recent years, the autistic community has begun to reclaim identity-first language. Many autistic advocates now prefer identity-first wording—that is, *autistic* or *autistic person* over *person with autism*. Throughout this book, I attempt to use the same terms that the teens use for themselves. In places where that is unknown or unclear, I have chosen to alternate between person-first (person with autism, student with autism, etc.) and identity-first (autistic person, autistic student, etc.) language.

By autism, throughout this book, I am referring to any of the disorders considered to be within the autism spectrum, including autism, Asperger's syndrome, and pervasive developmental disorder (PDD and PDD-NOS). During the long course of this work, even the definition of autism was in revision with the 2013 release of the American Psychiatric Association's *Diagnostic and Statistical Manual of Mental Disorders* (5th ed.; *DSM-5*), in which Asperger's syndrome was eliminated as a separate diagnostic category. This was much lamented by some people who identified with that label. I have attempted to keep intact the students' self-use of disability labels whenever possible.

Throughout the book, I relate stories about the youth and their lives, including some intimate and personal details that the students shared. The students and their parents or guardians agreed to allow their work to be used. In order to mitigate the risks of sharing such details, pseudonyms are used and some identifying details have been changed. In some cases, descriptions of the youth are altered or combined.

It was particularly difficult to capture the essence of photographs, video, and audio in a text format without compromising the anonymity of the youth. Instead of using the actual photographs, pictures are described in the text, as are video recordings. In the case of audio poetry, a medium that the teens used often, I transcribed the recording as closely as possible and used pauses in the audio to indicate new lines or stanzas. When possible, I asked the students themselves to read and edit the text version. For much of the student writing, I kept their original spelling, grammar, and spacing intact whenever possible.

One final note concerns the use of the word *teen*. Lesko's work (1996, 2012) around the cultural construction of adolescence problematizes the use of the term *teen* as rooted in a deficit understanding of youths and youth culture. The students in this book used the term *teen* to describe themselves.

I have struggled with how to name them as a collective without using the word *teen* while honoring the language the students used for themselves. Both *adolescents* and *youths* felt too formal, medical, or academic in this context. Although I use a more general *students* throughout, I sometimes kept with the term the group used most often: *teen*.

AUTOBIOGRAPHY ON THE SPECTRUM

Children, and people more generally, are builders, makers, speakers, creators. The making of works and work itself, are in large measure what we humans are about. Held within that wide embrace are what we know and name as identity, worth, recognition, and respect; and also, independence, livelihood, and vocation. Looking at children from this perspective calls attention to that strong desire to make—things and sense; a world and a life—as broadly descriptive of us as persons, as selves.

—Patricia Carini, *The Art of the One Loom*

"I swam too far in the sea and drowned"

A Different View of Autism

I'm a person that can do more than I seem like I can

People see me and they think oh,

Like fat person or different person who can't do anything who doesn't
    do anything,

Well I can do more than people think I can do.

—Charlie

In my first position in the education field, I taught in an autistic support program in an elementary school with children ranging in ages from 7 to 12. My students were technically listed as being in grades 2 through 5 because of their ages, but their evaluated academic levels ranged drastically. All of the children in my class were distinctly different, ranging in ages and abilities as well as language and academic levels, and no two children shared the same characteristics of the disorders that fall into the category called autism. My room was full of talented mathematicians, careful historians, and fanciful writers. My students could do many things: They played the cello, sang in the chorus, acted in school plays, or led morning announcements. Despite the medicalization and deficit standpoint of much of the literature on autism (Biklen, 2005; Kluth, 2003; Smith, 1996), my students were individuals with a great deal to share, as evidenced by a student in one of my first classes, Jenny, who wrote her autobiography several years ago:

My name is Jenny. I am 11 years old. This is story of my life.
    When I was born in december 14 my birthday is december 14. When I got the cards. I swam to far in the sea and drowned. Caleb and Sarah are here, when I was three years old. I am at the beach in Sea City. At Branton preschool I got my head stuck in the seat. I got in a car accicent with Jackie I hit a tree. When I was a little girl I got new beagel named Sugar at the Branton fair. Sugar is a new female dog is wearing a pink collar. When, I was little I went house back riding with Greg? I went on a picnic at thorncroffed with Sally and

1

Jack. At the old house in Brown street I meet Trish and Frank. When, I was little I went to Manhatten bagel with Sally, Charlie, Betty, and Ben?" When, I was little Sally yelled "go to my room!" When I was little I ran around at Aunt Kate's wedding and I take fresh air with my dad?" When I was little I watch Dumbo.

When I was four years old I went to Future Suns with Susan. I have a good day. I did not talk, when I was four.

When I was seven years old I got a new female beagel named Sugar is wearing a pink collar at the school fair and Sugar was born in April 14 at Branton school. I was so naked at the time out room and I peed on the floor. At lunch time I ate peanut butter sandwitch at Branton school and I thow up on the floor and I went to the nurse. I went on the lunch bunch with Mrs. Elias. I have going away party for me.

Before I worked with Jenny, I had not considered teaching autobiographical writing with my students. I had read much of the research on autism that was available at the time, and it was almost exclusively focused on the deficits associated with autism. Jenny, however, often told stories of her life and I began to encourage her autobiographical works. She wrote and drew the things that she experienced. She demonstrated very clearly that she could represent herself and her history. Jenny's work taught me a great deal about how children with autism can represent themselves through writing. In this work, Jenny told me many things about the people and places that were important to her. The piece of writing above, which I read early in my teaching career, showed me that Jenny, a student with autism and a history of communication and behavior issues, could make meaningful representations of herself and communicate those representations to an audience. I read Jenny in this piece, perhaps not exactly how she intended to be read, but certainly in a distinct way from what her educational history said about her. Jenny had good days like the school fair and getting a puppy, and bad days like the car accident. She loved her beagle and spending time with her dad. She overcame hardships and celebrated milestones. The file that came with Jenny from her previous school, however, presented low evaluation scores, a list of behavior problems, and a host of academic needs. Jenny constructed her own story in a way that demonstrated her capabilities, not just her limitations. It was with this first piece, and through close examination of this piece, that I began to formulate my ideas about students with autism and their identity construction through autobiographical writing.

THE PREVAILING DEFICIT MODEL OF AUTISM

Much of the current research on autism is framed within a deficit or biomedical/neurological model. In fact, the diagnosis of autism requires the indication of a "triad of deficits" encompassing social, communication, and behavioral skills in relation to what can be considered "normal;" the diagnosis of autism relies on a definition of typicality and a deviation from that norm (Biklen, 2005). The *DSM-5* (American Psychiatric Association, 2013) requires diagnosticians (usually psychologists or other members of the medical field) to consider a checklist of impairments and failures that are considered symptomatic of autism, including "deficits in social-emotional reciprocity"; "reduced sharing of interests, emotions, or affect;" "deficits in developing, maintaining, and understanding relationships"; and "persistent impairment in reciprocal social communication and social interaction" (p. 45). The *DSM-5* also explains:

> Deficits in social-emotional reciprocity (i.e., the ability to engage with others and share thoughts and feelings) are clearly evident in young children with the disorder, who may show little or no initiation of social interaction and no sharing of emotions. (p. 45)

Additionally, most studies of autism are centered on the pathology of autism, its causality, and medical or therapeutic treatments. From the first definitions of autism to the current diagnostic criteria, autism is considered recognizable by its subjects' deviation from the accepted norm. These constructs position autism as something "internal to the person" (Biklen, 2005; Smith, 1996) as opposed to a subjective reality that is open to interpretation in social, political, and educational spheres. Biklen (2005) explains, "Most of the language of the field assumes a shared, normative perspective of an observable reality. It is common in scientific accounts of autism to treat autism as more or less a relatively stable concept" (p. 11).

It is important to note that this deficit model is not isolated to an understanding of autism but is prevalent across the studies of disability. Pearl (as cited in Barton, 1998) points out, "Deficit thinking is deeply embedded in every aspect of American life. It is so much a part of the landscape that it is difficult to recognize, let alone address" (p. 61). The ways in which disabilities are labeled and addressed almost always rely on the negative and are "subject to institutional discourses of tragedy, medicalization, and otherness" (Priestly, 1999, p. 93). The deficit model of the medical community has a great impact on the language used to label students with educational needs (Biklen, 2005; Kluth, 2003).

In addition, many organizations are looking to "cure" (or prevent) autism, and it could be argued that their research further marginalizes those with the autism label. An Internet search of "autism cure" reveals more than 4 million hits, with links to sites about diets, hyperbaric oxygen chambers, stem cell therapy, treatment methodologies, books and articles, and even videos of "recovered kids." Advocacy groups such as the Autistic Self-Advocacy Network are pushing back, calling for the inclusion of the voices of people with autism. One website, created by an adult diagnosed as autistic, problematizes the search for a cure: "To cure autism is to eradicate people like me from the planet . . . to completely eliminate my kind" (Klein, 2001). Despite these calls, the dominant voice in autism research is not that of autistic people.

While the search for a cure falls within the medical field (with ideas that permeate education, community, and culture), the welfare or charity model emerges with the call for providing care for people with autism. In these two camps, Finkelstein (1998) points out, "The fundamental intention is to restore 'the impaired' to the greatest approximation of 'normality'" (p. 33). Again, these ideas are not only found within autism research but are part of the greater discourse on disability. Disability has historically been viewed and continues to be viewed as misfortune. This hierarchy of difference (fortune is superior to misfortune; therefore, normalcy is superior to disability) translates into a reigning "framework of charity and pity rather than equality and inclusion" (Devlin & Pothier, 2006, p. 10). This model positions individuals with autism as *less than normal*.

AN ALTERNATE VIEW: CRITICAL DISABILITY THEORY

The current deficit model used to define and research disability results in the "othering" of individuals in opposition to the societal concept of "normal." Problematizing this model, critical disability theorists contend that categories of disability (and therefore disability itself) do not exist outside of a social construct. As Devlin and Pothier (2006) explain, "Depending on what is valued (perhaps overvalued) at certain socio-political conjunctures, specific personal characteristics are understood as defect and, as a result, persons are *manufactured* as disabled" (p. 5). In this view, disability is not something internal to the individual but rather a byproduct of society's inability to view a range of differences as normal. The view of ability as a hierarchy is entrenched in the structures of society and is reproduced through institutions (such as medicine, education, and legislation). These structures disadvantage individuals on the basis of otherness (Devlin & Pothier, 2006).

Critical disability studies has joined other "post-liberal voices" (Devlin & Pothier, 2006, p. 9), such as queer theory, feminism, and other critical theories, in the call for a more inclusive social definition of "normal" and to push against the marginalization of those considered by society to be outside of that traditional definition. As Devlin and Pothier (2006) explain, "critical disability theory is increasingly concerned with targeting the problematic assumptions of the biological model in the distinct historical and institutional realms (of disorder and disability)" (p. 5). Critical disability studies is considered to be "the study of disabled people's lifestyles and aspirations" (Finkelstein, 1998, p. 32) in the wider context of the situated social constructions of disability (Devlin & Pothier, 2006; Finkelstein, 1998).

Instead of placing autism research within a deficit perspective, autism can be seen as socially constructed. Under the social model of disability, it is not the individual who is disabled but the society that does the disabling. In other words, social barriers such as an inaccessible environment, prejudice and discrimination, and inflexible social institutions render a person disabled. Consider one of Biklen's (2005) guiding principles for his book: "In order to begin to understand the person labeled autistic, as to understand any person, it is necessary to examine social context" (p. 67). In this view, autism can be seen as part of the larger societal construction of disability, yet labeled by a set of traits identified by society as abnormal. Autism is fluid and changing as social structures change and "may be seen as a set of qualities among many where the experience of the person can be understood only as being located and negotiated in complex socio-cultural contexts" (Biklen, 2005, p. 34).

Autism as a social construct is also an identity, one that is not all-defining or all-encompassing. Individuals with autism are, as all people are, multidimensional, a distinction often called for by the disability studies community. Singer (1999) takes these notions a step further:

> For me, the key significance of the "autistic spectrum" lies in its call for and anticipation of a politics of neurological diversity, or neurodiversity. The "neurologically different" represent a new addition to the familiar political categories of class/gender/race and will augment the insights of the social model of disability. The rise of neurodiversity takes postmodern fragmentation one step further. (p. 64)

Autism is often referred to as a spectrum disorder, one that can affect people in varying degrees. The label of autism, however, has more distinct boundaries: Either a person is diagnosed with autism or is not. Singer (1999) views the spectrum differently, allowing for all people to fall somewhere on this "neurodiversity" continuum. In critical disability theory, the label itself is situated in a broader social and political construct.

AUTOBIOGRAPHY AND AUTISM

Following the predominant deficit model of autism, a good deal of research in the field discounts the ability of an individual with autism to create personal narratives. In the book chapter "Taking It to the Limit One More Time: Autobiography and Autism," Smith (1996) explores claims that the neurological characteristics of autism "interrupt an autistic person's efforts to assemble meaning through narratives," stating, "In effect, the neurophysiological model consigns the autistic to an unautobiographical life" (p. 231). But what kind of a life is unautobiographical? This model implies that individuals with autism are not able to reflect on or share their self-histories. Despite these perceived limitations, Jenny (and other students like her) use autobiography to represent themselves in a complicated world. Jenny and I frequently exchanged stories to connect and cope in our classroom and in our lives.

Exacerbating this belief that individuals with autism cannot self-reflect is a notion put forth by Losh and Capps (2006), claiming that those with autism have limited emotional experiences. Losh and Capps conducted their study to examine the factors that limit the emotional narrative abilities of children with autism. They cite research that suggests that individuals with autism, in contrast to what was previously thought, can understand, label, and sometimes explain basic emotions. However, Losh and Capps put a limit on that understanding by saying that more complex emotions (such as embarrassment or pride) requiring self-reflection are elusive to autistic people. They cite experiments in which children with autism had more difficulty answering out-of-context questions about emotions than children not diagnosed with autism. Losh and Capps blamed the "inability" to construct emotional narratives on the underlying "emotional disability" of autism (p. 816). As a way to explain the issue, they state, "In other words, impoverished emotional experiences may leave little to discuss" (p. 816). They posit that it may not be the narrative-making that is impaired but the emotional experiences that are the basis for the narratives, or that people with autism somehow experience their emotions in such a limited way that they cannot make meaning from them.

Despite this research, there has been a relatively recent burgeoning of published works by autistic people themselves. Perhaps the most widely known is *Emergence: Labeled Autistic* by Temple Grandin and Margaret M. Scariano (1986). Grandin has reached a certain level of public celebrity, particularly for her autobiographical work and presentations on living with autism, as well as the HBO film based on her life that was released in 2010. *Emergence* is Grandin's first book, in which she details her childhood, adolescence, and early adult life. Grandin makes no apologies for the difficulties she had and often describes how she "overcame" these "problems." *Emergence* was published before the field of disability studies was named, and the writing reflects the dominant discourse of the time (despite being progressive compared to earlier studies of autism). In the foreword to the book, Dr. Bernard Rimland, a leading autism researcher of the time, described Grandin as a "recovered" or "recovering" autistic (1986). In fact, throughout the autobiography, Grandin refers to herself in much the same way. That Grandin would be able to "overcome the deficits" of autism to achieve success in her professional, academic, and personal life was considered an "escape" from the throes of autism.

Grandin's second book, *Thinking in Pictures: and Other Reports from My Life with Autism*, was written 9 years later, in 1995. In *Thinking in*

Pictures, Grandin continues to describe autism as it applies to her life but reconsiders her previous label as a "recovered" autistic. She acknowledges her differences from what is considered "normal," but demonstrates a level of acceptance of this. In fact, Grandin writes, "If I could snap my fingers and be nonautistic, I would not—because then I wouldn't be me. Autism is a part of who I am" (p. 16). Grandin's works were considered an anomaly in autism. Not only was Grandin able to self-reflect and share those reflections with others, but she was able to reconsider her own label over time.

Following the example created by Grandin's first book, other autobiographies of adults then considered to have "high-functioning autism" began to emerge. One author is Donna Williams, who has written several books about her life and experiences. Like Grandin, Williams reflects the dominant language around autism at the time of her writing. Her first two books, *Nobody Nowhere: The Extraordinary Autobiography of an Autistic* (1992) and *Somebody Somewhere: Breaking Free from the World of Autism* (2015), reflect the language of a person trapped by her diagnosis.

Like Grandin's first book, Williams's *Nobody Nowhere* also includes a foreword by Bernard Rimland. Again, Rimland touted the author as an anomaly in autism, an individual who was able to write from her own perspective "against incredible odds." He refrained from calling Williams "recovered," but represents her as "recovering." In his foreword, Rimland states, "Very few have made the almost superhuman transition from autism to near-normalcy" (Rimland, 1992, p. ix). Yet Rimland did not question the concept of "normal." Rimland also wrote that Williams's book served to illuminate the process of autistic recovery, explaining that Williams was able to begin this process through recognizing herself as "non-normal" and striving to overcome her autism. It is important to note that Rimland considered the writing of this autobiography part of Williams's recovery process, explaining that creating a chronology was the only way she was able to construct ideas about her identity. Rimland (1992) wrote, "We have known for decades that autistic persons experience life as an incoherent series of unconnected events" (p. xi). Rimland acknowledged the narrative writings of Grandin, Williams, and others, but only within the deficit framework.

Jenny's writing does not indicate that she had "an unautobiographical life," nor does it indicate that she had limited emotional experiences. Jenny wrote frequently, remembering details of her experiences and sharing them with others. She sometimes told her stories again and again, repeating stories to the same listeners until she was redirected to another activity. I was often struck by the stories Jenny had to share, stories about how she interpreted her world, stories about how the world interpreted her, and stories about personal challenges and triumphs.

Jenny is just one student of many who have shared their stories with me. In my classroom, and then in my work at a community-based center, many children have created their own space for self-discovery. I have worked with these students on our collective autobiographies, and 2 de-cades of experience with these children has shown me that they all have their own stories to share. This work raised questions for me about some of the assertions in the literature. Very often, the experiences in our group did not match the ways these students are portrayed under the tradition-al medical model. I have spent a great deal of time getting to know my students, and those relationships have allowed me entry into their lives. Although I am not a student with autism myself, my relationship with my students has allowed me to frame my teaching and my research as an outsider in collaboration with insiders (Herr & Anderson, 2005). Despite the fact that this work depends deeply on what I know about my students, it constantly reminds me how much I *do not* know about them. What we do not know about these students, and all students, is what makes this work essential.

I left the classroom to direct a center for autism services in a rural region of the United States. There, I frequently consulted with educators on the stu-dents with whom they worked. I also facilitated several programs for both adults and children with autism. One program that has become the focus of this book is the Teen Project, an after-school group for autistic adolescents. It is with this group that I set out to explore issues of identity and the ado-lescents' relationship with autism. Through the autobiographical works of the teens, I hoped to gain access into the opinions and perspectives of youth with autism, a viewpoint that is rarely considered in the field.

CREATING A SPACE FOR INQUIRY

The Autism Center, located in a small city in the United States, is a community-based nonprofit agency providing services to individuals with autism and their families. The center serves several large, mostly rural coun-ties that are among the poorest in the state. It is the only specialized autism provider within an hour radius; it is not unusual for children and families to travel an hour or more to receive services there. The Autism Center is also fairly new to the area. Prior to its opening, families in the area could access limited services through a regional cerebral palsy provider or through an-other disability service provider. Some families were able to access services in larger cities over an hour away. Families who had the personal means to do so often took their children to more metropolitan areas (over 4 hours away) for evaluations or consultations.

The Autism Center began counseling and school consultation services when it first opened. With a great amount of community support, the cen-ter and its staff grew quickly. The Autism Center now provides supports for individuals with autism across the lifespan, from preschool through adulthood. Groups at the center include a weekly session for autistic adults, a weekly group for teens, weekly and monthly parent/family groups, and social activities for children with autism, which are available several times a week. The center also created an inclusive summer camp for children and adolescents, and recreational programs include music, art, horseback riding, a drama workshop, and a swimming program. Consultations to area school districts occur on a daily basis to help support students in their educational settings. The Autism Center frequently hosts events to increase understanding about autism in the community, including workshops and trainings for parents, teachers, and other professionals.

The Teen Project

The Teen Project is a group for adolescents with autism that meets once per week after school at the center. Begun as a support-group pilot program, the group has shifted over time to become a kind of after-school club, a place for teens to spend time out of school with friends. Approximately 12 adolescents ranging in age from 12 to 17 were enrolled in the group at the time that is detailed in this book. The group was primarily male, with only two girls regularly attending.[1] Some of the youth were enrolled in their regular public schools, about half the teens attended special education programs, and two of the youth were not in school as a result of disciplinary removal. One teen in the group was home schooled.

The Teen Project was advertised through flyers distributed to local schools and counseling centers, as well as a direct mailing to families who had received services at the Autism Center in the past. Attendance is voluntary, and the teens are seen as an integral part of the planning process around the group's activities. Although it initially began as a support group, input from the group members caused the program to evolve into a multimedia expression group. I began with the hope that through the group, the teens would create some autobiographical writings, but this project also took on self-expression through photography, video, computer work, and music as well as writing and drawing.

The group met weekly on Thursdays after school. As with many youth, the adolescents in the group were dependent on parents or family members for transportation, and some of the teens were involved in other community activities; this often caused irregular attendance. On any given week, the group averaged about five students; some weeks, all 12 attended, and on one occasion, only two boys were present. Although the group met only once per week, many of the students came to the center more frequently, participating in other programs or just coming to "hang out," usually while their parents or family members accessed another service. The recreational spaces at the center are open at various times throughout the week.

Space

The group usually took place in a larger room often used for group space, positioned toward the back of the center. The room contains a long table with eight blue plastic chairs, a smaller round table with four additional chairs, a long set of shelves filled with toys and books, and an additional table off to the side stacked with bins of art supplies. A light blue rug, which the teens often point out is fraying at the edges, takes up about a third of the room; under it is a light tan tile floor. Off to one corner is a play area obviously for smaller children, with a preschool-size play kitchen and other toy items. In another corner is a large mat, about 2 feet thick, scattered with pillows and beanbag chairs for lounging. Two large windows line one wall; they look out onto a community garden and a small grove of trees. On the same wall as the door is a large two-way mirror that is covered with mini-blinds to maintain privacy during the group. The remaining walls are covered with art created by students at the center, as well as rules and reminders for other groups that are hosted there. For the Teen Project, there were typically three or four laptop computers set up around the room, and bins of electronic devices such as digital cameras, video cameras, and flip cams; accessories like camera chargers, memory cards, and thumb drives accompanied the bins of art supplies on the side table.

Depending on the size of the group and the activities planned for that day, the group sometimes spilled out into other spaces, including the observation room and counseling room in the same corridor. The observation room is a multi-use space on the other side of the two-way mirror; it was originally designed to house equipment and provide space for observations of therapy or evaluations. Although it does hold a television and recording equipment, the space has become a small kitchen with a mini-fridge and microwave and a storage room with two large cabinets of books and papers. The small counseling room is painted a soft yellow, with a red overstuffed chair and matching couch, a coffee table, and a patterned rug. A child's table and a staff desk are at the opposite end of the room. This room also has a two-way mirror for watching from the observation room, but this, too, is covered with mini-blinds and rarely opened for viewing.

On occasion, the group met upstairs in a large conference room in order to use the projector and screens there for viewing projects. In nice weather, the group met outside at a gazebo overlooking the buildings and a playground.

A Typical Day

Although the activities of the group could change drastically from week to week, a description of one session may help illuminate a general structure of the group. The Teen Project typically began at 4:00 P.M. to allow the teens time to arrive from their various schools or other settings. Because the rooms we utilized were in use throughout the day, the teens gathered in the lobby area to wait for the group to begin. Prior to the group starting, they often helped me carry equipment or materials into the back room and set them up, plugging in and starting up the computers or plugging the cameras in for downloading.

On this particular day, I walked down from my office to the lobby of the center. Six students were there, all male, two accompanied by waiting parents; a few were talking raucously about a recent local basketball game. I pulled equipment out of a cabinet behind the reception desk and asked several of the students to help me. As I handed out materials, the teens carried them back to the group room and began to set up, still chatting along the way. Back in the room, they followed the usual protocol of plugging in and turning on the laptops, or arranging the chairs and work spaces as they liked them. During this time, one other member, a female, joined the group while apologizing for being late. Each teen brought a group-issued camera or video camera, and many plugged their cameras in for charging or downloading to one of the laptops.

We gathered at the long table for a discussion of the plan for the day, which we had decided at the beginning of the month would be a project workday. We then brainstormed as a group the stations that the teens wanted to work in, decided who would begin in each station, and reviewed the activities of each station in a guided discussion (see Figure 1.1). The group set 15 minutes as the general shift time so they could access the majority of activities in the allotted time, with time at the end to spend on their overall projects or at a station where they wanted additional time. It was agreed that I would float among the stations to help with technical issues during this session, but during other sessions, I might participate in creating my own project.

Figure 1.1. Stations on a Typical Day

Station	Space We Used	Supplies
Blogging	Long table in common room	Laptop, scratch paper, pencils
PowerPoint	Smaller round table in common room	Laptop, thumb drives where projects are stored, scratch paper, pencils
Comic drawing	Art table in common room	Plain paper, comic-strip templates (available for free online), pencils, markers, colored pencils
Audio self-recording	Observation room with chairs	Digital audio recorder or tablet, scratch paper and pencils
Partner video interviews	Small counseling room with chairs, couch	Handheld digital video camera or tablet, scratch paper and pencils

The group then spent about 10 minutes reviewing all of the stations, a discussion that I guided (see Figure 1.2 for guiding questions). Once all the stations were set up, each teen went to one section and began working, with two students going to the small room to collaborate on an interview session with each other. I kept the time, and every 15 minutes the teens switched to a new activity.

Each transition took longer than planned, and in the end, there was little time left to wrap up. Many of the teens stayed late to save their projects and help put away the equipment. We resolved to spend time during the next session presenting and discussing what had been worked on during this meeting. After all the students had been picked up, I spent time writing notes about the session, downloading the audio and video to my computer, and transferring projects and data from the other laptops and thumb drives to my own.

Collecting Stories: The Use of Personal Narratives

The Teen Project continues to be an ongoing project of the center, but the work detailed in this book lasted for approximately 1 year. During that time, the adolescents and I met weekly as a group to work on their multimedia projects. During the year, the teens had opportunities to write,

Figure 1.2. Guiding Questions for Stations on a Typical Day

Station	Guiding Questions
Blogging	What do you want to blog about today? How do you log in to your blog? What are some things to remember about blogs? (Blogs are public, we don't post identifying information like names and addresses, and so forth.)
PowerPoint	What have you been working on so far? What aspect of your life story do you want to tell today? Can you add one additional slide today? Can you add photos or graphics to your story?
Comic drawing	Do we want to work on a particular theme? What are some comic-strip features (word bubbles, sound effect words, and so on) that might be helpful? How can you show a beginning, middle, and end?
Audio self-recording	Do we want to explore a particular topic today? What are some ideas? How can you prepare before you record? Would it be helpful to make yourself some notes of key points? How long should your recording be? How do you start, stop, and save?
Partner video interviews	How do you focus the video? How do you zoom in, and how far? What kinds of interview questions might you ask? How do you start, stop, and save?

draw, photograph, videotape, and compose about their lives. Each week, the group was given the materials for a piece of the multimedia project that they chose and self-directed. I anticipated that the teens themselves would spend time discussing how and why to use each mode; I would assist in facilitating these discussions and provide assistance as needed. As each piece was created, the teens would have the opportunity to share and discuss their works with the group.

I focused on the study of autobiographical works, which make it possible for individual differences to be negotiated and reframed in the contexts of personal experience situated within the larger structures of society (Biklen, 2005; Gee, 2000). Gee (2000) further explains the view of personal narratives as a key to understanding others:

> People make sense of their experiences of other people and the world by emplotting them in terms of socially and culturally specific stories, stories which are supported by the social practices, rituals, texts, and other media representations of specific social groups and cultures. (p. 2)

Narrative is a way to retell experiences and recraft relationships; what stories are told and how they are told are always dependent upon the social contexts in which the stories are situated. Autobiographical accounts, when viewed in the broader social context, can serve to illuminate an individual's actions and the societal influences that mediate those actions. When people are given the opportunity to describe, from their own point of view, their history, actions, and reasoning, they may make visible the context in which their personal history occurred. Although not always explicit, social influences are always present. Additionally, narrative work allows individuals to contribute purposefully to the construction of their own social identity through self-representation (Blackburn, 2003; Campano, 2007; Carini, 2001; Cole & Knowles, 2001; Thomas, 1999; Wilson & Lewiecki-Wilson, 2001).

I initially envisioned group activities focused around autobiographical writing, much like the work I had done with Jenny and her classmates. The teens, however, deemphasized more traditional modes of writing in favor of multimodal works, to include a variety of digital media. Using these tools was a constructive process for all of us in the group. I did not set out to include digital media, but as the group evolved, it became clear that this inclusion would increase engagement for many of my students. Those in our group usually selected the modes they wished to use to portray their stories. During one early group meeting, the students brainstormed a list of ways in which to tell a story; these ranged from practical (for example, write the story) to whimsical (create a puppet show). Some of the ideas were current for their particular social group (show texts to tell the story or turn the story into anime), whereas other ideas were farfetched or impractical (e.g., train a parrot to tell the story). A list produced by their brainstorming session is included in Figure 1.3.

The teens often used drawings or comics, photographs or posters, and video and audio to tell their stories. During one session, one student even used his computer to retell a story in Morse code. I began to rethink what I was counting as autobiography, what was an act of literacy or reading or writing or communicating, and what I could/would count as an artifact of this experience.

As the Teen Project morphed over time from a support group to a recreation group to a self-exploration group that combined support and recreation, I began to see the opportunities for practitioner inquiry within this new work. I had long admired the work of Mollie Blackburn, a practitioner who explored identity work in an afterschool project with LGBT youth.

Figure 1.3. Ways to Tell a Story (Brainstorming Session)

Reenact the story
Write the story
Make a movie
Burp out the story
Tell people about the story: audio or video
Puppet show
Train a parrot to tell the story
Draw a picture of the story
Talk about the story
Use sign language or charades to tell the story
Write a play about the story
Do a voice-over, have someone else record the story
Show pictures of the story
Sing a song about the story
Rap the story
Slideshow
Show artifacts, like a show-and-tell
Make a poster about the story
Make a dance about the story
Make up a fictional story based on the real story
Interview people who were there
Show texts to tell the story
Retell the story to another person and have them tell it
Write the story in code
Make a comic strip
Turn the story into anime
Make a movie and narrate what happened
Turn it into a game of telephone
Print images about the story
Have someone ask questions about a story

Blackburn (2002, 2003, 2005) examined literacy acts as agents for social change. I had always hoped that the work I was doing could provide a similar space for these types of acts, albeit with a different, yet still marginalized, group of young people. Once the group was under way, I began to see its potential as a setting for inquiry. I discussed these thoughts with the youth themselves, and they were very open, even eager, to this idea. They, too, saw potential in the work we were doing and hoped it could contribute to the larger conversations about autism, ability, and the concept of "normal."

The following chapters (Chapters 2, 3, and 4) investigate three main themes that the youth took up in the autobiographical works: representations of home and family, explorations of school experiences, and considerations of the disability label, respectively.

CHAPTER 2

"The walls of my room"
Representations of Home and Family

Billy spoke about the walls of his room in his audio poetry. Cody detailed the measurements of the walls of his home in his audio work. Trevor took pictures of the outside walls of each house he lived in. Lacey showed all the walls in her home in a video tour she created. Charlie photographed the crumbling walls of an abandoned barn on his family's farm. Walls were most evident in this theme, particularly when the youth were representing images and ideas about their homes and families. Their works provided entry into their lives, access to a personal understanding that only each teen could build.

During the yearlong span of the project described in this book, the group of students created hundreds of autobiographical pieces for their collections. By autobiographical, I mean focused on their own life experiences, which included family members, friends, school, and representations of their interests. I consider all of the pieces created by the teens to be autobiographical in some way, as they all represented their interpretations of their lives in the world around them. They used a range of media, including photography, poetry, writing, drawing, singing, and audio and video recording. Modes of choice often depended on the youth's level of comfort or experience. Although modes like photography and drawing were used more frequently than others, all the teens utilized multiple modes throughout their projects.

The students, very different individuals with unique experiences and perspectives, nonetheless reflected shared themes in their explorations. In our work, one of the most common topics that surfaced was an exploration of home and family. This chapter examines the ways in which the youth took up this topic in their works. I take a deeper look at one student's works and use examples from others to explore two broad themes that were predominant in their representations of home and family. The first is that the teens demonstrated understandings of people in their lives and their relationships with them; they offered an awareness and critique of their own experiences and showed a connectedness to the people around them. They also held expectations of the ways in which people are supposed to act, and they incorporated these expectations into their representations. The second theme is that the youth used their works to claim agency over and make sense of experiences in which they perceived themselves as lacking power; they created representations of home as a place of both security and vulnerability. They also reflected on judgments about themselves and others, and they used their work to explore and sometimes deflect their own feelings about these judgments.

The chapter begins with a look at one student, Billy. I selected Billy for this chapter because he created representations of home and family that illustrate his complicated history in ways beyond what might be expected based on his clinical diagnosis. I also selected Billy because I was deeply moved by his work. He created many pieces on this topic of home and family, and he took on his own history very directly despite a subtlety to his work. I'm acutely aware of what Adichie (2009) calls "the danger of a single story"—the problems of a singular image that can stereotype and define a whole group—so I offer these images of Billy's representations as an alternative to the common wisdom about youth with autism. This is intended as a counternarrative to the majority of the images put forward in the literature.

Billy's works are juxtaposed with selected pieces from the rest of the group, which I include to make clear that concerns about home and family were not unique to Billy. Even though all of the students explored the topic of home and family, their projects were very different, emphasizing the notion that any one group has many stories. The thematic threads of interpersonal connections and struggles for power were common to all the projects.

OPENING UP: AN INTRODUCTION TO BILLY

First Impressions: Billy, His Dad, and His Background

When I first met Billy, he was 15. He was sitting next to his dad in the center's reception area listening to an outdated, portable CD player. Billy had been coming to our center for about a year for counseling sessions with a social worker. He was always accompanied by his father, who struck me as a gentle but persistent man; every time he saw me, he asked how he could get additional services for his son. Billy himself was tall for his age, with the beginnings of facial hair growing in patchy spots and wire glasses hanging unevenly on his face. He was dressed in a typical teen outfit of faded jeans and a sweatshirt depicting the logo from a local college sports team.

Over the next few years, I saw Billy and his father frequently at the center, usually in the reception area while they waited for Billy's therapist. The center also provided Billy's Medicaid service coordination, so they met monthly with a different social worker to arrange services. I saw Billy and his father at social events and fundraisers held at and for the center, and sometimes his stepmother attended these as well. About once a month, Billy's father came to a parent group, sometimes with Billy's stepmother and sometimes alone.

I occasionally met with Billy's father in my office, usually to hear his concerns or requests. Once, Billy's dad complained about a local sandwich place that donated food for one of our fundraisers; the owner had asked Billy if he had autism, and Billy's dad found that presumptuous. On several occasions, Billy's father came to me to request scholarships for Billy to attend certain groups or for him and his wife to attend a workshop or conference. Once, Billy's dad came to me to request help obtaining a used car in order to transport Billy to and from his various activities.

When we first started to publicize the Teen Project, Billy was the first one to sign up. "This is what we've been waiting for!" explained Billy's dad as they handed in his application. As I looked through the paperwork, I saw that Billy's father had filled out the entire packet and it appeared he had done so without Billy's input. Throughout the application, Billy's dad described him as very affectionate and very sensitive. He also wrote that Billy liked videogames, couldn't run or do any contact sports, and needed help with social skills and making friends. Billy's dad listed his son's diagnosis as "PDD-NOS," a nonspecific category at the time within the autism spectrum. One thing that struck me in particular was a note on the bottom that read:

> Never bring up his birth mom. When he talks of mom, he is referring to his stepmom. We have sole custody. Birth mom found trying to assault Billy with knife. He's very sensitive about this. Misses his half-brother; better to avoid conversing with him about this.

This caveat made me a bit nervous. I immediately worried that this topic would come up in the kind of exploring I had hoped the youth might do in this group. I was concerned that this would be a bigger issue than I could help navigate, something better left to the social workers or psychologists we had on staff. I also worried that the topic would come up in Billy's work and his father would be angry with me for allowing it, but I knew that I wasn't going to make any topics off-limits in our group.

I met with Billy and his dad to talk about the Teen Project and my vision for what I hoped the group to be. During that meeting, Billy and his dad explained a bit about Billy's diagnosis and his background. In his early childhood, Billy had developmental delays characterized as severe: He crawled, walked, and spoke his first words after ages that caused concern with his pediatrician. He was classified as having a developmental delay and received early intervention at home and at preschool. Upon entering elementary school, Billy was reevaluated and diagnosed with autism. Once he received this diagnosis, Billy was placed in a special education classroom. Billy also has a heart condition that limits his ability to engage in vigorous physical activities.

Billy moved to the area with his father and stepmother when he was 9. Before that time, he lived in a large city several hours away with his mom and his younger brother. He had not seen either since his move years prior, but Billy did occasionally visit his aunt, who still lived near his previous home. Billy's father has a physical disability and has been out of work for over a decade, and his stepmother is a refugee who speaks little English. She has a daughter who at the time was in her late 20s; Billy considers her his sister. Billy and his parents live in a two-bedroom apartment above a barbershop approximately 20 minutes from the center.

Billy's Participation in the Teen Project

Billy took his role in the Teen Project very seriously. At 18, he was the oldest member of our group, and he participated in the project during his last year of high school. He attended almost every week and was the most regular participant of any of the students. He took meticulous care of the equipment he borrowed and did every assignment the group created, even if it meant a lot of work outside of group. For the few sessions that Billy missed, he came to the center beforehand and turned in his equipment and work with notes about why he would be absent.

During the course of a year, Billy collected a large body of work for his personal autobiography. He submitted close to a hundred photos. He created more than two dozen pieces of writing, several drawings, and 15 videos. Billy also created a blog that he posted to from both the center and home. Billy's work often focused on relationships, particularly at home and at school. He also expressed feelings about his early life, his relationship with his parents, his difficulty making and keeping friends, his desire for a girlfriend, and his hopes and plans for his future.

During one of our early sessions, I posed the following question to the group: "If you were going to tell the story of your life, what would you include? How would you tell it?" I was hoping to get the teens brainstorming about what to create for their projects. We had already discussed ways to tell a story, and now I was prompting them to consider using those modalities to tell their own histories. Most of the students filled one or two pages with a list of life events or personality traits they considered important. Billy also created a list that was a mixture of events, places, people, and traits, and next to most of the items, he proposed a way to tell each story (Figure 2.1).

I see this list not as an exhaustive catalog of what Billy considered important in his life but as a snapshot of what he thought of himself and his own history during one brief work session. The list even reflects a joke that was just told in the group (Cody's purposeful mispronunciation of the word *purple*) that I doubt Billy would even have considered had the list been written on a different day. It was a contrived exercise, not one I intended to gain serious insight into the teens' inner thoughts. I had only meant it

Figure 2.1. Billy's Initial Autobiography List

My Life:

- Laughing at cody's favorite color "purbk"I mean "burple"
  I mean "purple"! (chat with him and put on video)
- Birth-know already (video)
- School-been there, done that (pix of year)
- Grandparents from both sides- be with them(pix)
- Dad — interview (write out)
- "Stepmummy" I mean "step mamaw" I mean "step mom"
  I mean "step mother",-Be teacher and student(drawing)
- go wednesdays (video)
- Garner (write out)
- Living in studio apartment (video)
- Deploma student graduate (write out)
- Hard worker (Drawing)
- Flirter (video)
- Lovable (video)
- caring (video)
- Seeker (write out)
- Loving music (power point)
- I ove movies (pix)
- math smartie (video)
- fighter (write out)
- Soccer star (video)
- Bowler
- God parents.

as a starting point to get the teens thinking about how to make their own representations.

Billy did use the list to prompt some of his later work. He ended up showing pictures of school, interviewing his dad, making a slideshow presentation about music, and writing about a fight. Some of his proposed modalities changed during the project; Billy took pictures of his apartment instead of a video, and he wrote about his stepmother instead of drawing her. He created lots of works covering topics not on this list, and left out many of the items listed. He also experimented with other ways to tell his story, and incorporated some of his listed personality traits into other pieces.

When I first read Billy's page, I wondered how many things on this list were really how Billy saw himself and how many were how he wished to be seen. For example, Billy listed "soccer star" as one of his items and even proposed a video to portray this. But Billy never created a video of himself playing soccer, nor did he show any pictures or create any stories of himself as an athlete. As previously mentioned, Billy's father had listed on his application that he could not run or do contact sports as precluded by his heart condition. Billy did, however, discuss sports as a possible profession for himself several times in his work. In one self-led audio recording, Billy expressed his wish to play sports:

I told my dad I'd like to be a teacher
I figured I'd love being a teacher 'cause I was good at math
Or maybe I'd be a tutor
Or a substitute
Which is a helper,
But I gave up on that hope.
So I said, a teacher's job is not gonna be for me
Or maybe a sports job would be.
So I figured either, I figured I'd join the baseball team
Um a baseball team in the MLB, in the majors,
Then I quit.
I figured I'd join the NFL
Then I gave up on that.
So then I came to basketball and then soccer,
So I'm stuck between those two.
I'm firmly considering doing basketball
Possibly, and soccer
And soccer's my second choice
But um
I really hope that
I get what I would like
Which would be for me to show my parents how physical I am
How physically active I can be

In this recording, Billy first considered a career in teaching but then abandoned that wish for a career in professional sports. He seems to have considered several different sports before settling on basketball and soccer. Billy did not, however, seem interested in professional sports for the same reasons many other teens do; he did not mention multimillion-dollar contracts or national fame.

Other labels Billy gave himself may have been reflections on his desires as well. I see Billy's understandings of what is expected for a young man his age coming through in this work. Billy listed certain attributes such as "fighter," "flirter," and "gamer" that might not be how he saw himself. Throughout the year, it became apparent that Billy, although he liked videogames, did not have a videogame system at home and did not have any experience with the types of games avid fans his age enjoyed. I don't think that any of the other teens would have described Billy as a gamer, although there were others in the group whom they may have described that way. Billy also shared one experience in which he was "beat up" at school, but his account positions him as the victim, not the fighter. In fact, Billy's sensitive nature as well as his eagerness to please others puts the label of fighter at odds with the rest of his list.

Throughout his time in the Teen Project, Billy engaged in identity work in naming himself and his experiences. He built connections to others through his work and explored the relationships in his life. In his work, Billy expressed expectations he held of himself and others. Throughout this process, he and the other teens took risks by both revealing and hiding themselves, and sometimes by placing themselves in positions of vulnerability.

MAKING CONNECTIONS

In the beginning of the year, many of the works Billy created were about his special interests. He brought in photos of wrestlers, his pets, or objects that were important to him. At first, the photos told a superficial story of his life. He focused on items he liked or interests he had, but did not spend much time creating pieces that showed his deeper experiences or feelings. As Billy became more comfortable with the group, he began to create representations of his family and friends. In one picture, Billy and his father were posed in front of a pool table, each holding a pool cue and standing shoulder to shoulder, smiling for the camera. In another, Billy photographed his stepmother as she unpacked groceries in the kitchen of their apartment. These pictures began to provide a glimpse into Billy's life and to reflect relationships with those he cared about.

Beyond these pictures, Billy really began to show deeper views into his life through his audio recordings. Often, one of our group stations consisted of a digital recorder and several pieces of paper. Occasionally, the group decided beforehand on a particular topic, such as "What is the best thing that ever happened to you?" or "Friends at school," but most times they left the topic open. The teens could spend some time sketching out ideas on paper or they could go straight to the recording. For the first several months of group, Billy avoided the topic of his mother, referring only to his dad and stepmom when referencing his family. Eventually, the subject of Billy's separation from his mother did surface in his work. Billy first chose to explore this topic in a piece of audio poetry. During one taping, Billy recorded the following:

I heard a noise outside of the walls of my room
Where I was sleeping with my brother
The door opens up to our room
And there's our mom
Our mom had a knife in her hand
I knew who she's going after
She was going to go after me
I suggest you go to the guidance counselors
Your son's coming in
Smelly
He doesn't bathe every day
He wears the same clothes every day
What am I to do?
The guidance counselor literally drew him a big picture
My guidance counselor drew him a big picture and said
Custody and
Over me
The judge saw what was happening
Yes, your honor, as a matter of fact I do
She kept coming for a couple weeks
Then stopped
The judge was just
Making me more pain
Putting me in more pain than I was already in
After that the judge said
Mr. McQueen, you're absolutely right
Nothing of the sort
At all.

When I first listened to Billy's recording, I was struck by its heaviness. I felt Billy's presence in it and was moved, especially since I recognized that this was Billy's first time sharing a representation of his mother in his project. In it, Billy explored a distressing event from his childhood, recounting the experience that caused his mother to lose custody of him. Billy made decisions about how to represent this experience, and his personal reading of the event is apparent throughout. This representation would be vastly different had the same events been recounted by another person, such as Billy's dad or brother or the judge. This artifact is more than just a story or recounting of events for an audience. Billy engaged in difficult work confronting his feelings and memories of this experience. He explored and represented complicated social relationships throughout this piece.

Billy displayed a connectedness with others in this piece. In each stanza, he is not alone. At the beginning of the poem, for example, Billy is with his brother. Billy's brother is only included in the very beginning of this piece, and Billy did not reveal many details about him.

But what Billy left out is just as important as what he included. By saying, "She was going to go after me," Billy implied that his brother was not attacked. We see this again later in the piece, when Billy said, "Custody" and "Over me," which also left out his brother. This implies that only Billy was attacked and that his father filed for custody only over him, and not his brother. Billy implied that they were treated differently because the story shows the guidance counselor only expressing concerns about Billy. It could be that Billy's brother was not in danger or it could be that Billy's memories of the events are only the ones that pertain to him. Billy began to explore his connections to others and their connections to one another.

Later in the year, Billy created a video in which he talked about missing his brother. Billy related in this piece that he cries every year on his brother's birthday because they are not together. Birthdays, he shared, are especially difficult because they used to celebrate together as a family. Every year, he finds that the time he misses his brother the most is on either his birthday or his brother's. He said in the video, "The birthday came around again. It was very hurtful that I couldn't be with my brother." Billy also explored his relationship with his brother during the short amount of time that his mother had visitation rights. He said that he asked his mom to bring his brother so they could hang out together, but when his mom stopped visiting his brother did, too.

This work can be considered in contrast to Gallagher's (2004) notion that persons with autism lack intersubjectivity, impacting their ability to understand the connections between people. For Billy to create this piece, he displayed an understanding of his connection to his mother, his brother, his father, his guidance counselor, and even the judge. He explored the thoughts, intentions, and actions of others. In fact, Billy demonstrated a deep feeling of regret over his separation with his mother. This provides a stark contrast to the stereotype of individuals with autism as self-isolating. The strength of Billy's connectedness is reflected throughout his work.

Billy's feelings about his parents were not always static, and this was evidenced in his work as well. Once, Billy blogged about visiting his grandparents in Austin (see Figures 2.2 and 2.3).[1] In the first entry (Figure 2.2), Billy was excited that he was going to visit his old hometown, but he expressed that he would miss his relationship with his parents while he was gone. A week later, Billy posted a contrasting entry (Figure 2.3). His trip was canceled, and he was disappointed that he wouldn't be able to go. In this entry, he did not write fondly of his parents but described himself as "stuck" with them.

Billy's feelings about his parents changed with his experiences and circumstances. Variation of experiences, and interpretation of these experiences, is what Erickson (2010) calls a personal "heteroglossia." He explains that "Each person's life experiences differ somewhat from those of other

Figure 2.2. Billy's Blog Post About Visiting Family, 4/13

> **tuesday, april 13**
>
> I am going down to Austin to be with some friends and family
> (me amigos y familia). I will miss being able to talk with my mom
> and dad (me madre y padre). As I move to Austin for a visit I
> always say, "I will miss being with everybody that I know of
> from up here." That is a fact that can and always be proven.

Figure 2.3. Billy's Blog Post About Visiting Family, 4/22

> **thursday, april 22**
>
> I am very depressed in not being able to go visit my friends and
> family in Austin (mi amigos y familia) and I am sad to be stuck with
> my mother and father (mi madre y padre). I'm really glad though
> that I am with my teen group

people, and every person lives in a variety of social situations each day. Differing social situations provide differing ecologies of relationships with other people" (pp. 50–51). Heteroglossia does not create conflict within the multimodal autobiographies but instead provides a richer and more complete picture of the students' personal histories.

EXPLORING RELATIONSHIPS

The stereotype of autism is one of isolation, what Biklen (2005) calls "the myth of the person alone." The pieces the students created, detailed in the following sections, provide a very different picture. All of these teens, youth with autism, undertook the task of exploring relationships. They examined their own traits through their connections with others, and they illuminated the complexities of their families and showed an understanding of others that pushes the boundaries of expectations about autism.

Exploring Relationships with Parents

Billy was not the only one in the group to take up the theme of relationships throughout their projects. In fact, the most frequent subtopic the students explored was the subject of parents. Each of the teens took up some work about his or her parents at least once in the work. Many students took pictures of their parents at home, and several included photos of themselves with their parents. (Only one did not photograph his parents.) Parents were also a frequent subject of conversation in the group and became a common topic when the teens interviewed one another in audio or video clips. For example, Cody used his video work to show the struggle between reliance on his parents and his wish for autonomy. He reported that he got along with his parents "okay" and that he had the hardest time when his mom was nagging him, which he said was "always and about everything." Cody felt that his mom was too involved in his life and was home too much; he wished that she would work more hours so that she wouldn't be around him as often. Cody's project became a space for him to explore his thoughts about his family. Like many other teenagers, Cody experienced the stretch of exploring his desire for independence while maintaining the safe environment of his home and family.

This process of individuation is common to teen narratives, as youth work to establish themselves as independent yet connected (McLean, Breen, & Fournier, 2010). In constructing their personal identities, the students struggled with this desire to separate from their parents. They often addressed points of conflict in their relationships with them. Carson, for example, discussed his relationship with his parents on his audio recordings. He said that although he liked mostly everything about his parents, he had trouble with them "on rare occasions." This was usually, he admitted, because he kept pushing his parents about things he had been anticipating for a while, like when they would get a new pet or go on a vacation. Carson showed that he understood how his actions could influence his relationship with his family, and that he sometimes caused strife in his family.

These relationships were apparent through all of the teens' works about family. Mark often discussed his parents in his work and addressed issues of relational conflict. He reported a close relationship with his mom, but often wrote about how his relationship with his dad was strained, particularly since his parents separated. Mark included one picture of his parents together in his collection. In this picture, a young Mark, approximately 6 years old, sits at a picnic table holding an ice cream and smiling for the camera. He is flanked by his parents. It is, he told the group, the only picture he has of his parents together. All three people in the photo are smiling, and Mark expressed in group that this was when his family "used to be happy." His relationship with his parents, as well as his parents' separation and divorce, became a main subject for Mark's project. Mark took up the work of exploring his parents' changing relationship in their family, and he used his project as one way to delve into this complex theme.

Exploring Relationships with Siblings

Sibling relationships were another prominent topic for the teens. Works about siblings often overlapped with those about parents, extended family, or blended families. All the teens in the group have at least one sibling, and most report that their relationship with their sibling is a significant part of their lives. Some of the teens wrote about younger siblings and their varying friendships with them, as well as times when they do not get along. Some of the teens wrote about older siblings who no longer live at home, and some presented photographs or videos of visits to those siblings. Carson, for example, described his brother as his opposite. He viewed his brother's rambunctiousness in contrast to his own calm demeanor, and his brother's messiness in contrast to his own need for order. He was able to examine his own traits through his relationship with his brother.

Exploring Relationships with Extended Family

Many of the teens also created works about extended family. Several took photographs of grandparents, aunts, uncles, or cousins. Some created videos, like Rachel, who recorded a game of hide-and-seek at her cousin's house, or Trevor, who recorded his grandfather's birthday party at a nursing home. For some of the teens, the significant role of extended family in their lives was reflected in their work. For example, Mark featured his grandparents in more than 10 pieces of work, describing the role that his grandparents filled after his parents' separation. Cody described his cousin Allan in more than one piece, explaining how Allan came to live with him and why Allan could no longer live with his own parents. Extended family, for some of the teens, featured as prominently in their projects as their immediate family. This exploration of who and what counts as family shows a connectedness to others that is largely absent in the stereotype of autism.

Exploring Relationships in Blended Families

Over half of the students in the group live with a stepparent or stepsiblings, and some of them created rich pieces that take up the topic of blended families. In one video recording, Charlie tried to make sense of his family relationships, wondering if his half-sister could be his stepsister if their parents never married. He also explored how he could feel closer to his older stepsister than his younger half-sister, as he saw the fact that they were "related by blood" as an indication that they should have a closer relationship. In another piece, Charlie saw his siblings as taking sides with and against each other. When talking about his stepsiblings, he said, "We lived together. We'd always fight because we never got together well with either one of them.

It was like a war zone. Me and my brother would always face them. They would stick together and me and my brother would stick together." In these pieces, Charlie interrogated his relationships with his siblings. Carson also created recordings in which he talked about his half-brother and struggled to understand his father's prior relationship. This topic of blended families can be a complicated one, and it was discussed frequently among the teens during group time. They often pondered the difference between stepsiblings and half-siblings, or discussed family alliances, disagreements, or complications like split holidays.

EXPECTATIONS: THE WAY THINGS ARE *SUPPOSED TO BE*

The students did some sophisticated work exploring their own assumptions about family as well. Billy, for example, held certain expectations of "how a family *should* be," and he explored these beliefs in his project. In one audio recording, Billy said:

You think that a family's supposed to be
You think a family would always be together
My mother
Separated me from my brother

In another audio recording, Billy shared:

It's sad
Because, you would have thought that
A mother would have cared for her own son
Because that was her young and
She just gotta help raise it and help make it stronger

In these pieces, Billy showed he had certain expectations of how a mother takes care of her children. He had experienced something different from these ideas and he struggled to make sense of what happened. During the group and in his body of work, Billy never provided a reason for his mom's actions, and he never directly asked why she treated him as she did. Billy had a vision for how a family should act, and that vision was at odds with his reality.

In stark contrast to his relationship with his mother are Billy's reflections on his stepmom. In one piece, Billy wrote about when he was young and needed to have heart surgery. He wrote that his stepmom was critical to his recovery: "She wanted to be there to support me 100 percent all the way and I got better because of her and my dad. But my real mother that I used to live with never came to visit me one time." He also wrote that his stepmom moved to the United States in order to get medical care for her daughter, Billy's step-sister, who was critically ill at the time. Billy credited her with saving her daughter's life, sacrificing all they had to become refugees. Billy mentioned his stepmom in several pieces of his work, usually in a very positive light. By contrasting his mother and his stepmother, Billy revealed the disappointment he felt when his mother did not live up to his expectations.

Other students used their projects to interrogate their assumptions about family as well. Charlie explored his expectations about family in a video recording of himself. In this video, he talked about his brother:

My brother is hyper, annoying. But he's annoying in a good way, annoying in the way that sometimes you really wish he'd go away, but it's his personality. You just love him to death, but you don't really show it to him. You fool around; he might think you don't like him, but you actually do. He thinks I don't like him but I really do. Little brothers are supposed to be annoying to older brothers, [it's] the way it goes. Little brothers are annoying; older brothers are somewhat mean, but I'm not really that mean.

In this piece, Charlie explored how his relationship with his brother both fit and defied expectations. He expected his younger brother to be an-noying, and saw it as his brother's role in their relationship. Charlie viewed his role as one of the tough older brother, but admitted that he was not real-ly that mean, or as mean as he thought older brothers were supposed to be. Charlie almost did not want others to know how much he liked his brother, or perhaps he did not want his brother to know it. This struggle between sibling alliance and rivalry was reflected in many of the collected pieces. Another set of pieces by Charlie explored his relationship with his youngest sibling, a 3-year-old half-brother. He and Charlie share the same father, but the father was no longer in a relationship with either of their mothers. He and Charlie had never lived together and had only seen each other a few times. Each visit was prompted by Charlie's mother; Charlie ex-plained in one of his video interviews that his mom got the children together once or twice a year, even though she did not know either the little boy or his mother. Charlie was particularly confused by this relationship and explored it in more than one piece, including a video he created, an audio interview with another teen, and a piece of writing. For example, Charlie wondered aloud in a video recording if he was his brother or not, since they rarely saw each other. He questioned the definition of a sibling, saying, "He never sees us, we never see him, so we can't really be considered . . . I mean there's always that blood thing, but what's the point of being considered if you never see each other?" In one piece, he stated that he should do some-thing because he is his brother, but in another he said that they're not really siblings. In these examples, Charlie used the autobiographical works to ex-plore his relationships and the expectations he holds about family.

In another example, Mark blogged about a sacrifice his sister made that he judged as "heroic": After his father offered to send just one of the three children to Arizona for a trip, his sister refused to go without her siblings (see Figure 2.4). This piece explores both the strained relationship Mark experienced with his father and the alliance he felt with his sister. Mark judged his father and his parents' divorce as the cause of their missed family vacation. The piece has a strong sense of right and wrong, ending with an indignant statement by Mark's sister. In this short piece, decisions were made by Mark's father, Mark's sister, and Mark himself. It also reflects a sense of responsibility to family. Mark judged his father to be responsible for his disappointment. At the same time, he applauded his sister for acting on her responsibility to her other siblings.

There was another side to the theme of expectations in the students' works as well. In a few of the pieces, the teens examined their diagnoses (and themselves) as responsible for some hardships in their families. Their interpretive frameworks for autism will be taken up in a later chapter, but autism was also represented within the theme of expectations for family. Billy addressed it on a few occasions, especially in terms of how his disability affected his family's finances. Mark blamed his diagnosis for how hard his mother must work to provide for his education and needed therapies. Charlie directly linked his autism as responsible for his parents' divorce. In one session, while Charlie was showing a photo of himself at his mom's wedding to his stepfather, another student, Anthony, asked Charlie how he felt when his mom got remarried. Charlie clearly struggled with his answer, restarting a few times and trailing off in others: "Uh, I felt nervous. 'Cause I didn't know how it was going to go through. I felt, like, I felt like I don't understand why she left my dad in the first place. 'Cause . . . I, I love my dad, but . . . things happen, I guess."

The group was silent for a moment, and then another student, Rory, asked, "What things happen?" Charlie was faster with his response this

Figure 2.4. Mark's Blog Post Illustrating the Alliance He Felt with His Sister

---

april 1

If it was not for my father and this whole divorce we would be in Arizona right now basking in the sun having a vacation. He thinks that it would cost him too much, (We Would Not Even Be Using His Money) for us to go to Arizona this year. He even offered to send one of us (out of the 3 children) with his parents to Arizona. My sister looked him in the face and said "We go together, or not at all!"

time: "Fighting . . . people dying in the family, stress, have a kid or something like me and my brother. And it gets kind of tough and stuff. [Long, audible sigh] Breaks a lot of stuff, spirits, family relationships and stuff."

The group was silent again, this time for a longer amount of time. I knew that Charlie's brother was also diagnosed as autistic, and I tried to clarify if that was what Charlie was referring to. I asked, "So, are you saying that having a kid like you and your brother caused some of the issues your parents had?" Charlie replied:

Yeah. Well, they always, when I talk to them, they usually say that the other one didn't do anything to help us. Like, my mom will say my dad didn't do much to support us when we, when we were there. But my dad will say that he did a lot and that she didn't do anythi . . . that she didn't do a lot. Where I remember them both doing a lot, but they kind of blame each other.

Then Elizabeth, whose parents were also divorced, said, "They should stop blaming each other. 'Cause blaming each other is just what little kids do."

In this dialogue with one another, the youth explored their expectations of how parents are *supposed to* act, as well as Charlie's feelings of responsibility for some of his parents' arguments. They constructed their ideas about family relationships together and grappled with their thoughts about relationships gone awry. They also examined how they played a part in their family struggles. This type of causal thinking is contrary to much of the literature about autism, which proposes that autistic individuals have difficulty constructing cause-and-effect relationships, particularly in cases where emotional understanding plays a part (Losh & Capps, 2006). In this example, Charlie and the other teens made connections that were steeped in emotion and based on understandings of personal relationships.

The students took up the theme of expectations in a variety of ways, exploring the duty of family members to one another, their responsibility to their families, and the effect of their diagnoses on their relationships. This thread carried throughout the works on home and family. Instead of viewing themselves in isolation, the teens saw themselves as responsible to and for the well-being of their relationships. They saw themselves as an integral part of their families.

TAKING RISKS: TELLING VERSUS NOT TELLING

Creating these works, as is often the case with sharing personal histories, was a risky endeavor. The youth sometimes struggled with what to tell and what to leave out. They demonstrated a self-consciousness that is common in sharing deeply and personally. We worked as a group to create safe spaces for sharing, respect the multiplicity of identities that each teen brought, and respect the risks that others took.

Creating a Safe Space

On one particular afternoon, we had planned time for the group to share pieces of their autobiographies. As was usual for these sessions, I began by providing some basic reminders about giving feedback, which always included something about being respectful and honoring the work everyone had done. When I asked for a volunteer to show his or her project first, Rachel timidly raised her hand about halfway but said, "As long as I can leave the room while you watch." I asked if she would want to stay in the room in case we had questions, and Rachel compromised by volunteering to stand in the corner of the room while her video was presented.

I asked Rachel to tell the group about her piece. Rachel explained, "This is about how I got inspired to do fan art." She gave a brief definition of fan art, and then explained that she chose to create a rap, but that it was a video for everyone to watch. Rachel then cued up the video and went to stand in the corner of the room with her back to the group. The video was about 1.5 minutes, and was an audio recording of Rachel rapping, accompanied by photographs of the art she had drawn with a ticker across the bottom explaining the photographs. The rap itself consisted of rhyming lyrics to a beat that Rachel created, which told a story of her beginnings in fan art. She rapped that she had seen fan art done by a friend, and decided to then try it herself. After the video was over, the group clapped, and Rachel returned to her seat, smiling but partially covering her face.

Before Rachel reached her seat, Anthony exclaimed, "You should post that on YouTube!" and several people, including myself, told Rachel she had done a great job. I said, "Rachel, this is excellent," and Rachel responded with, "This is just what I do on a regular basis at home." I then asked why she had chosen to rap about the experience. She crossed her arms but smiled slightly and replied, "I don't know, it was somethin' different. I like to be different." Several group members nodded in agreement or support. Billy added, "That's cool." I pressed Rachel for more details, asking, "What do you mean, you like to be different?" Rachel explained, "Like, I just like to do stuff that's a little out there, like not, people aren't really expecting. Plus, I purposefully disagree with people sometimes. To avoid being cliché." I reiterated that I liked her project, and then asked if anyone in the group had feedback for Rachel.

Billy started off. "Those are nice drawings," he offered. "They look like the actual, like what I can see in a video." The rest of the group began asking Rachel some technical questions, like what program she had used, how she had put it all together, and how she timed it. Then I asked, "Rachel, why did you pick this particular story to tell?" Rachel thought for a few seconds, then responded:

Maybe because it has the most to do with my life. I was going to choose a different one, the night where I spent 8 and a half hours in a friend's apartment, and it was really crazy. I just wanted to talk about a sort of journey. It involves that night, sort of. And another night. 'Cause, I just wanted it to be a long story, made a little shorter.

I then asked Rachel if I could share her project if I disguised her identity. Rachel agreed, saying, "I'd be cool with that. Just if you hear any laughing, that's to be expected." I addressed the group, saying that sometimes when we perform something about ourselves, we might feel a little self-conscious or embarrassed. I asked if anyone else felt that way. Anthony responded by saying, "Well, if you do a good job, it could be a tiny bit awkward, but it was good." Then Rory asked, "I have a question. What do you mean *embarrassed*? Like, what do you mean, someone would be embarrassing?" I elaborated with an example about myself feeling embarrassed to sing in front of other people. Anthony seemed to support my example, saying that of course it would be embarrassing to sing in front of my students, but that I could sing in front of others. I said, "Well, I'm not a professional singer, so it might be something awkward or embarrassing for me. I might still do it, but I might feel a little embarrassed." Rory, animated as though he suddenly understood this concept, said, "Like when we talk about the reproductive system in health, and it's embarrassing. You can't say that in front of public people, like I'm not gonna say that in front of the whole world." Cody then jumped in with, "Yeah. Like they're not even sure what that's supposed to mean."

Anthony added, "Like it can be embarrassing what I can do. It can be a little funny. Say that if I get on this tape and I dance around like a disky[2] boy. That could be embarrassing." Rachel, who had been quiet for most of this discussion, replied, "I would never do that in school. Just here in group, and even that was hard." Most of the teens nodded, and a few said "Yeah," or "I know." Cody offered, "It feels like, if you maybe do something unusual, you can get embarrassed from that." Billy, who hadn't spoken since his first comment, added, "You know what I think is, um, brave? It's that Rachel thought this would be embarrassing, but she did it anyway."

This vignette exemplifies how the youth built themselves into a community of creators. They shared their projects and the intentions of their work. The students gave one another feedback and explored their understandings together. They took risks in this sharing, and recognized and honored this risk-taking in one another. Through this community building, the teens were able to create the group as a safe space in which to construct their identities.

Rachel was specific about this when she noted that she could expose herself in group in ways she wouldn't in school. The teens established group as a safe space for exploring, sharing, and responding.

The students also explored emotions together in this piece. Salient here is the feeling of embarrassment, an emotion that Losh and Capps (2006) specifically name as elusive to individuals with autism. Self-conscious emotions like embarrassment or pride, they explain, require reflection on the internal thinking of others. They claim this capability is lacking in people with autism, which ultimately affects their capacity for expressing complex emotions. This example directly counters that claim. The teens may have shown some difficulty in naming the emotion, but this example shows that they could certainly experience, remember, and relate the feeling of embarrassment. In fact, they could also recognize the feeling in others and support one another in exploring those emotions.

Being different was a source of pride for Rachel but only in ways that she controlled. She expressed that she liked doing what was unexpected and didn't want to be cliché. At the same time, she was embarrassed to watch her own performance and was nervous about how the group would react. This risk-taking that the teens did in the group was impacted by their fears of being judged. Even those who embraced some types of feedback seemed to show a level of embarrassment about opening themselves up to critique.

Multiplicity of Identities

What the students chose to represent in their projects often reflected their level of comfort in the group. They made deliberate choices about their representations. These choices, like the projects themselves, were not made in isolation but were informed by the social contexts in which they existed. The youth were well aware of their audience, a group of their peers, and they often edited their work accordingly. Billy, for example, had spent the first few months of group leaving out as much as, or perhaps more than, he included. When interacting with the group, however, he appeared self-confident, happy, and often funny. He shared many private jokes with the other group members. Most of these I was not privy to, but I observed the giggles and whispers the teens shared. Some of these moments were even caught on camera by the students themselves, pieces I found when I was cleaning up files on my computer or clearing space on the digital camcorders. In one such clip, there is a short video close-up of Ivan. While I watched it, I heard Billy's voice calling Ivan's attention, revealing him to be the photographer of the clip. Billy recorded Ivan rocking in his seat and then turned the camera on himself, whispering, "We're getting up close and personal here." Both boys laughed loudly.

When Billy was the only one in the room, however, his demeanor was often serious. It was only in those moments that Billy chose to explore some of the more difficult experiences of his life. In these more private moments, Billy unabashedly admitted to acts and events that he did not describe in group. In one video, he described an experience of being bullied at school, an assault that was so severe he had to be taken to the hospital. In another work, Billy detailed a day when he ran away from school, only to be picked up by the police and returned to his father. These were a few of the pieces that Billy created that he did not share with the group.

The multiplicity of identities, what Phelan, Davidson, and Yu (1998) refer to as *students' multiple worlds*, requires an adept ability to transition, especially for adolescents. It is revealed in what the youth chose to include and exclude. These decisions show a sophisticated understanding of audience. It is so sophisticated, in fact, that the students altered their own identities based on their audience. Billy concealed aspects of himself for group, especially initially, in order to protect himself. All of the youth explored their multiple selves: The person they presented to the group (like Billy and Ivan's video), the one they presented in school (as in Billy's stories), the self at home (like Rachel's fan art), and more. Yet it was not only location that determined the shift of these multiple selves. The students had multiple identities that they enacted in a variety of social situations, ranging from powerful to vulnerable.

Risky Identity Work

The identity work that the youth engaged in could sometimes be risky, even in a small and intimate group like this one. In one piece, Carson made this sense of risk explicit as he told only a partial story of his family finances. He talked about how the family's credit cards were at their limits, and how his father's job "ran out of work for him." Carson also talked about how his family rented out their house when they couldn't make payments on it, and when the renters stopped paying, they were stuck paying for both their house and their apartment. Suddenly, however, Carson ended the discussion, saying, "There's some things you can't know. You could get into a struggle if you knew about that. We're already in enough stress, financially. And also, rumors spread really fast." In this recording, Carson expressed that there was something he didn't want to talk about because it could cause trouble for his family. He felt his family was already experiencing enough difficulty with finances and he didn't want to burden them further.

After listening to this piece, I reminded the students that if there were things that they wanted to keep private, they didn't have to share them with the group. Although I wanted this group to be an outlet for them to discuss their experiences, I didn't want any of the teens to feel pressured into sharing something that could make them feel more at risk. Carson had expressed a sense of responsibility to his family, and he had concerns that he might put them at risk with information that he held. Despite any protections that would be made, the youth were often able to recognize the risks of telling their stories. This is not expected if only considering their diagnoses, as autism is often seen as an inability to take another's perspective (see "theory of mind" research). However, Carson's story above and many of the others demonstrate strong understandings of outsider perspectives.

LOCATING SELF

Through this process of crafting a personal history, Billy took an active role in his experiences. He and the other students wrote and read their own personal histories, interacting with their own stories in a way they hadn't before. Through this reading and writing, the youth were, as Beach and Bruce (2002) describe, "engaged in processes of formulating issues and questions, investigating, creating, discussing, and reflecting" (p. 154). Billy's telling of his own history was both empowering and risky (Goodman, 2003).

Locating Self Through Vulnerability

As these were autobiographical projects, the students put a good deal of effort into centering themselves in their works. This centering, however, often placed the teens in very vulnerable positions. In Billy's earlier piece of audio poetry, for example, he used his work to make sense of an experience in which he was not afforded much power, an experience that could be very difficult to relate. Billy utilized several conventions to protect himself in this work. For example, he changed the sense of perspective several times throughout the piece. In Billy's poetry, the suggestion to go to the guidance counselor seems to be from a perspective other than Billy's own. We can't even be sure who is being addressed, as it could have been a suggestion to Billy or to his dad. Then the question, "What am I to do?" appears to be from Billy's father's perspective. The last stanza contained pieces of a conversation in court that does not seem to include Billy. In these ways, Billy discussed himself from a distance. He did not say, "My mom stopped showing up and this caused me a lot of pain." He instead framed this abandonment from the perspective of others and the court. This can signal, as Grotevant and Cooper (1998) theorize, a high level of connectedness, which they describe as two-dimensional. This connection requires two parts: response to others' views and accounting for others' viewpoints.

This distancing also makes Billy seem almost disembodied in this piece. He provided some details of what happened in this experience and his understandings of those memories. The story is told in a way that separates Billy from the experience, despite his presence in the piece. He could have said, "My mom stabbed me with a knife. I was bleeding and screaming and I was so hurt. My dad finally realized I was being neglected and he filed for custody. I went to live with my dad. My mom had visitation rights for a while but she stopped showing up, which really hurt me. Then she lost visitation rights, too." That would have been a more conventional way to tell the story, but it would have left Billy vulnerable to talk about his memories and how he felt. Instead, he told the story in a way that distanced himself from the experience. The use of other perspectives may have allowed Billy to deflect feelings of pain, sadness, and abandonment.

Billy also explored his experience through the use of repetition. This may have served as another way Billy emphasized his thoughts, as though these repetitions signal the moments that Billy struggled with. For example, "our mom" is repeated in the first stanza. The two sentences "And there's our mom" and "Our mom had a knife in her hand" paint two very different pictures for the listener, causing the audience to suddenly reframe what is happening. The repetition makes it seem as though Billy struggled with this realization as well. "The guidance counselor drew him a big picture" was repeated in the third stanza. Billy remembered that the guidance counselor expressed concerns about neglect. By saying that the guidance counselor "drew him a big picture," Billy implied that this was something obvious; however, it could also be that Billy was not familiar with this idiom. He repeated it twice, perhaps to try to make sense of the expression, and he used the word *literally*, as though an actual picture were drawn. Another example of repetition is "more pain," which was repeated in the last stanza. Billy said, "Making me more pain. Putting me in more pain." He rephrased this slightly in the second instance, emphasizing the deep feelings of his experience.

Billy also may have used this piece to claim agency over his experience by assigning the cause of pain to the least personal character, the judge. In his recording, Billy described an experience filled with pain caused by neglect and abandonment. The agent of these circumstances was Billy's mother. Throughout the piece, however, Billy never assigned the cause of pain as his mother. In the first stanza, he didn't place blame on his brother as a bystander. He also didn't implicate his father or guidance counselor as sources of pain despite their inability to protect Billy, nor did he blame them for the ensuing custody suit. It is not until the last stanza, when Billy's mom stopped attending her visitations, that Billy addressed the pain he was in. Even then, Billy assigned the pain to a neutral agent, the judge. This may be Billy's way of dealing with the hurt inflicted by those he cared about the most. By assigning his pain to the judge, Billy could deflect the blame from those he loved.

It was not always clear how much of Billy's stories came from his memory and how much was Billy's retelling of his father's (or another person's) telling of the stories. From the audio poetry, it is not clear if Billy was in the counselor's office or in the courtroom to overhear these discussions or if he received the information secondhand. Either way, it had become part of Billy's personal truth. Receiving information from trusted authorities like teachers or parents, what Goodman (2003) calls *local interpreters*, can help fill in the holes in a personal history. Sometimes in our group, the students asked me a question or tried to clarify a happening from a story they told. Sometimes they asked one another, and other times they reported what a parent or teacher had explained. Particularly when recounting events from early childhood, or events that had a social context that may not have been clear to the students at the time, the youth may rely on these local interpreters to make sense of their stories.

Locating Self Within One's Place in a Family

Billy worked purposefully in his project to locate himself within his small current family but removed from the family of his past. As previously noted, his larger body of work includes pictures of his dad and of him and his dad together. It does not, however, include any pictures of his early childhood, his mom, or his brother. In only a few audio interviews did Billy mention his parents' divorce, or that his mom lost custody of him when he was young. In one self-recording, Billy said that the worst thing that ever happened to him was "being stuck with someone who didn't care for me as much as I thought they did." Occasionally, Billy's pieces mentioned his mom, but these usually referred to his stepmother, not his biological mother.

Whenever Billy discussed his future plans in our group, he always considered his father and stepmother. When Billy wrote about his future, he usually expressed that he wanted to get a good job to support and remain close to his parents. In one journal entry, Billy wrote, "College will be good because I will be able to get a very good job to support my mom and dad because I would like for them to be happy for what I am doing and become very proud of me." He felt a sense of responsibility to his dad and step-mom, and those feelings were reflected in his images of home and family. Sometimes, Billy related that he wanted to become a professional athlete and in other pieces an accountant, a bank teller, or even a teacher. Especially in these works about his future, Billy often considered his family's finances. In one self-recording, Billy said, "I'd have to worry about how much money I'd do. My dad's worried about money as a bank teller. So, uh, I don't know what I'm going to do yet." Billy thought about his future income when considering his career choices.

During one discussion about money, Billy talked about how his family is eligible for certain public disability benefits. He said:

It's kind of hard for me to do this, to do work. So, and I, I also get SSD (Social Security Disability) and SSI (Social Security Income) checks sent to me. But my dad, my dad is my payee for them. He, uh, spends the money to buy my clothes. He spends it to buy my food. He spends it to pay the rent, pay the electricity, the heat, the water, the garbage, everything. And he also pays taxes at the school. And thank god he's been doing that.

During the time that Billy was in group, Billy's SSI checks and his father's disability payments were the only sources of income for their family. On their application to receive free or low-cost services at the center, they listed their annual family income as well below the poverty level. Despite his anxiety about finances and his sense of responsibility for his family, Billy was very optimistic about his future. He saw himself as someone who would have the power to change his family's situation. Billy also did not see his disability as limiting his career choices. As noted previously, Billy often spoke about his career aspirations. In some pieces, Billy discussed becoming a professional athlete. In another piece, Billy wrote that he was studying to become an accountant, which would help him support his parents and stay close to his family. He wrote that his plan was to live at home to save money while he attended community college for 2 years, and then to attend a large private university about an hour and a half from his home. Billy also said that he wanted to be an accountant so that he could wear a business suit and go back to Austin to file for visitation rights with his brother.

By describing his story, Billy made public his private feelings of fear and abandonment. Billy's history won't change; his experience with his mother is set in his past. Billy's talking about that history, however, changed in this process. Our group became a safe place for Billy to reclaim authority over his own experiences. Billy's work began to change to reflect a sense of action and of intent to direct his own future.

CLAIMING OWNERSHIP

Billy stopped coming to group when he graduated from high school. Perhaps it no longer fit into his schedule, perhaps he felt that he was too old, or perhaps he lost his transportation as his father had been anticipating. I still see Billy on occasion, and he always wants to tell me something he finds interesting in his life. Billy is now enrolled in a special education program at a nearby community college. He just completed his first year, which he reports on with great pride. Billy still lives with his father and stepmother, but does hope to have his own apartment in the near future; he feels that finances are the only reason preventing him from more independence. He still does not have a driver's license, but wishes to buy a motorcycle someday. Billy hopes to be reunited with his brother before his next birthday, but doesn't know how likely that is to happen.

Throughout his work, Billy made decisions about what life experiences he wanted to represent. He used his values and beliefs to make choices about how to express his experiences. Each teen chose artifacts for different reasons and prioritized their life experiences differently. These are simultaneously private and public works (Gee, 2000; Pahl & Rowsell, 2006) in that they explore personal understandings and make those visible to others. They represent particular identities, values, beliefs, and understandings for each teen (Young, Dillon, & Moje, 2002). These projects, created by the teens and co-created by the group, are more than a collection of artifacts from each individual; that is, they represent each individual's struggle to create an identity to present to others.

In their research, Losh and Capps (2006) found that only some individuals with autism were able to construct narratives, and even that work was limited to conveying simple emotions. They question not only the ability for individuals with autism to relate their emotions, but the depth of emotional experience for these individuals as well. Losh and Capps point to "deficient emotional knowledge" (p. 816) for their findings of inadequate narrative accounts. Yet the youth in this group recounted deeply emotional experiences across all their bodies of work. They constructed a space for sharing those accounts and ways in which to support one another's creations. The students pushed the boundaries of what was expected of them based on their diagnoses.

Throughout this work, the teens displayed an intricate understanding of their family relationships. They presented these understandings as they examined their own expectations of home and family and created narratives around these topics. The youth used these narratives to make sense of their experiences and to explore their own locations within those experiences.

The walls the students depicted represented safety and danger, security and vulnerability. These images of walls can be seen as a metaphor for the worlds in which the youth lived. There were walls that the teens built up around themselves, protecting them from painful memories or from making themselves vulnerable. These walls were present in the stories that were told and even more present in the stories that went untold. Sometimes, the walls represented the limits of what the students revealed. They separated themselves with these walls and defined their own space for exploration. At the same time, they constructed walls around the group, creating a safe space in which to work together. In the following chapter, we will see ways in which the youth used these safe spaces to explore the sometimes unsafe world of school.

CHAPTER 3

"I hope school starts to calm down so I can too"

Enduring, Resisting, and Reframing School Experiences

Throughout the year, the topic of school figured prominently in our inquiry group, a purposefully out-of-school experience. Many of the youth experienced oppressive forces in the school setting, as detailed throughout this chapter. This after-school group was intended to be a safe space in which the youth could come together to explore their experiences. The teens in the group formed a community of practice outside of school in which they positioned themselves vis-à-vis school. The following vignette, which describes one of the first significant conversations about school that arose in the group, demonstrates the beginnings of this collaboration.

One Thursday afternoon, the students gathered in the large upstairs conference room. I had prepared the space by positioning the tables in a U-shape to facilitate some group interaction while allowing everyone to view the screen in the front of the room. As the students came in, I asked them to download their new pictures onto my computer. One by one, the teens came in and got settled. Charlie, always wanting to be the helper, made hot chocolate for everyone at the kitchenette in the back. All of the students found seats at the tables and chatted with one another.

The last one to arrive was Elizabeth, who came to the door with her father. Elizabeth had dark eye makeup smeared on her face. She was clearly crying and hesitated at the door for a few minutes before saying good-bye to her dad as he left. She went to an open seat between Cody and Trevor without saying anything, sniffling slightly. As she sat down, I offered gently, "It looks like you're not having a great day, huh, Elizabeth?" She nodded but didn't speak. I asked if she wanted to just sit and relax for a while, and she mumbled yes. Cody passed Elizabeth a copy of the afternoon agenda. Then he whispered, "Everyone is taking a pencil and a pad of Post-its to write down things we want to remember" as he passed her the box of supplies. Elizabeth nodded, took her items, and proclaimed aloud, to no one in particular, "I really hate school." Cody responded in agreement, saying, "Yeah, we all hate school. I'm treated like a hobo. A retarded hobo." Trevor laughed loudly, and a few others snickered. Cody retorted that this was serious, asking, "Can't you see that Liz's having a hard time?" Everyone got quiet, and Cody encouraged Elizabeth to tell what happened. Elizabeth offered, "School isn't fair. They say I'm not in trouble, but they have to call my parents anyway." The group was indignant. Trevor said, "Why? That doesn't make any sense!" Cody, pausing carefully, asked, "Why were you in trouble?"

Elizabeth then told a story about a boy in her new class asking for her phone number and her not telling the counselor because he would get in a lot of trouble. Another teen, remembering that Elizabeth had shared the week before that she had been expelled from school, asked a question about her new school. A few of the group members said something about how unfair school is, talking in dyads or small groups. Ivan, who was sitting alone at the far end of the room, expressed aloud, "I wish I could go to school."[1]

Throughout the year, the youth brought their school experiences to the group and to their projects in various ways. They shared their observations with one another and incorporated stories of school into their projects. The teens explored these school experiences, and many of them found ways to reinterpret their histories. Some of the students related pieces about academics, but more often, as illustrated in the above vignette, they investigated experiences of personal and social difficulties. Their stories changed based on who was listening and asking, and sometimes the accounts changed as the teens grappled with their own feelings about an experience. Many of them depicted school as a hazardous place filled with bullying, misunderstandings, and struggles.

The previous chapter explored how the teens made connections to family and their expectations of those relationships. We saw the youth taking risks in their writing as they struggled to locate themselves in their own narratives. I proposed that through these works, the students began to claim ownership over their own stories. In this chapter, I examine the works of three students to show a range of ways they responded to their school experiences. The youth, working together in this after-school program, became a kind of inquiry community. By this, I mean that the students were committed to exploring and learning together (Cochran-Smith & Lytle, 2009; Wenger, 1999). Through this collaboration and using their works, they created connections to one another. They learned about themselves through and with one another as a community. Building on the claims of ownership from the previous chapter, I show how the teens began to "craft an agentive self" through this collaboration (Hull & Katz, 2006).

Through these works, we get to see an insider perspective of the school experience as it is interpreted by the students themselves. This is critical work because much of the current literature about the experiences of children with autism in schools comes from a medicalized or rehabilitative perspective. In today's political and educational climate, children are increasingly labeled by their test scores, their ability to perform on standardized measures, and how they compare to norm groups. In special education, the 2004 Individuals with Disabilities Education Act (IDEA) mandates an individualized education program (IEP) for every identified student, which must identify the student's needs and address each one in annual goals and benchmark objectives. Through these mandates, students' educational experiences are divided into discrete pieces to be measured and addressed; this is a clear example of the emphasis on a deficit model at work in education.

Perhaps of even greater importance is the fact that schools serve as *socializing institutions* (Barton, 1998) that can have great influence on the reproduction of current knowledge, maintaining the status quo, or alternatively, identifying, acknowledging, and pursuing other perspectives. Placing education in the forefront of the discussion about disability discourse is "about far more than disabled people; it is about challenging the oppression in *all* its forms. . . . It is impossible, therefore, to confront one type of oppression without confronting them *all* and, of course, the cultural values that created and sustained them" (Barton, 1998, p. 59). Schools, as part of the greater context of social value reproduction, can hold tremendous responsibility for addressing oppression and, ultimately, change (Barton, 1998; Biklen, 2005; Peters, 1999).

In addition to the larger societal picture, schools can have tremendous influence on the development of self-identity in its pupils. People with disability encounter different levels of inclusion or exclusion in their educational environments, and many adults have spoken out about the obstacles that prevented them from fully accessing academic instruction (Biklen, 2005). Levels of inclusion and exclusion, blame and accommodation, teacher expectations, and student acceptance all have impacts at both the societal and individual levels (Barton, 1998; Biklen, 2005). Very little has been written about these school experiences from the perspective of children with autism. Despite the drastic increases in the numbers of school-age children with autism (from 1 in 150 in 2000 to 1 in 59 in 2018, according to the Centers for Disease Control and Prevention), their voices remain on the margins if they are recognized at all.

IMAGING AND IMAGINING: LOOKING OUT AT OTHERS LOOKING IN

On the day that Elizabeth came to group in tears, we had planned to watch a documentary together as a group. The short film, titled *Outside/Inside* (Waltz & Pentzell, 2002), features a man with a developmental disability who communicates with the use of a keyboard. The film is approximately 7 minutes long and shows some clips of the main character's typical day, such as visiting a convenience store. The video is accompanied by the text he typed about his life, which scrolls across the bottom of the screen. In the film, the main character describes himself as very different from the way others see him.

We watched as a group, everyone quiet with their eyes fixed on the screen. No one took notes or commented during the movie. After the film, the students also had very little to say. I called attention to some of the text the main character had written. I asked the group if they could select some ideas communicated in the film that resonated with them. After some persuading, the teens chose three items from the film as writing prompts, which I typed up and handed out to the group. The phrases chosen were as follows:

1. On the outside I look _____.
2. I see myself as _____.
3. People treat me like _____.

The students spent a few minutes silently writing, filling in the blanks independently. I gathered all the responses in a pile, and we talked for a bit about how we might incorporate some of these ideas into our projects.

Afterward, we had planned some time for the group to share the photos they had taken the previous week. However, I had a feeling that many of them were still thinking about the conversation with Elizabeth from the beginning of the session, so we decided to forego the original plan of photo sharing and spend some time creating based on the film prompts. We quickly set up two stations, one for drawing and another for audio recording. The youth split up, picking a place to work and working mostly on their own. Elizabeth drew a comic strip of a negative school experience in which she regained power (investigated later in this chapter). Others drew pictures or doodled, and some took the audio recorders into the hall or adjoining rooms to spend time recording. Both Billy and Carson expressed their own experiences with marginalization at school. Billy recorded:

Some of the kids and the teachers in the school, most of them
Treat me like I'm not wanted there
And that really hurts. . . .
In school, you got all the jocks, you got all the geeks, and you got all the nerds,
    which are geeks as well.
Question is, who would I prefer to hang out with?
I'd probably say, none of them. I'd rather be by myself.

Carson recorded:

Some teachers just accept me for who I am, despite the sometimes trouble that I cause. And some, some just can't get over it. Well, I don't know why they say this, but they consider me annoying a little much. . . .

I used to think I was bullied, but I'm kind of getting used to it now, from hearing it so many times.

These pieces, in which Billy, Carson, and others shared glimpses of their feelings of marginalization at school, were the first surfacings of what later became a consistent theme addressed by the youth in our group. Although the documentary we viewed was not about school, the themes of isolation and flawed assumptions prompted the teens to take up the topic of school in their works. This particular session, from Elizabeth's entrance to their writing prompts and their station work, was one of the first times the students addressed school frontally. It also marked the beginning of their collaborative work about school.

The members of the group shared common experiences but interpreted those experiences in a variety of ways. Often, the students examined their feelings of isolation and outsiderness. They explored how they were viewed by others and sometimes contrasted the assumptions of others with how they saw themselves. The three youth highlighted in this chapter all brought stories of oppression from school to group. By oppression, I mean experiences of prolonged and institutionalized distress. I also mean experiences in which the teens were rendered vulnerable or powerless by an external structure. Despite the common experiences of isolation and maltreatment, the three students in this chapter all took up this struggle in different ways. Some built stories of endurance or resistance, whereas others created new histories for themselves. As I will show, this exploration and collaborative work regarding these experiences became a means for them to assert agency.

CHARLIE: ENDURING OPPRESSION

Situating Charlie Within the Group

In response to the prompts that the teens and I had made together after watching the film, Charlie made three bold assessments of how he saw himself and how he thought others saw him (Figure 3.1). He perceived himself like other kids but felt he was treated as an outsider. This was the first time in group that Charlie referred to the bullying he experienced. This piece initiated a dialogue for Charlie that focused on his encounters with persecution.

My first experiences with Charlie came during the summer before he entered 8th grade. At the time, he was attending a summer day camp run by the center, a program we set up as a recreational and social alternative to summer school.[2] Charlie was big for his age, rather tall and heavyset, with blondish hair and fair skin. He was in the oldest group with seven other campers and three counselors, all college students employed by the center for the season. I saw Charlie as a conscientious youth: His attendance at camp was perfect, and he set it as his own mission to keep reminding everyone about sticking to the rules. However, the other campers occasionally

Figure 3.1. Charlie's Response to Three Writing Prompts About How He Views Himself and How He Thinks Others View Him

Name: *Charlie*

Date: *12/16*

On the outside I look
Like any other Kid.

I see myself as
A Normal Kid.

People treat me like
I don't deserve to be an earth.

complained that Charlie was bossy. I also viewed Charlie as a peacemaker, because he was uncomfortable with disagreements within the camp and often took it upon himself to broker accord. He also seemed to jockey to be the counselors' favorite, and he considered many of the adults to be his friends.

The following year, Charlie and his family began counseling at the center, taking part in a group session every other week, and he attended nearly every social event the center held. The next summer, Charlie again came to camp, giving himself even more of a leadership role based on his previous experience there. He often came to me with suggestions or complaints, feedback on his counselors or other campers, and comments on activities, schedules, or trips. I knew from what Charlie and his mother had told me that Charlie was struggling in school and that they were looking for additional social experiences for him for during the school year. When we began the Teen Group in the fall, I was sure to send Charlie the packet of information. Sure enough, Charlie was one of the first that year to sign up.

Throughout the year, Charlie continued as a self-designated rule-keeper but often faded into the background during loud group interactions. He put himself into a helper role whenever possible, volunteering to set up and clean up the room, do everyone's downloading, or assemble snacks or drinks for the group. He sometimes got very rambunctious, bouncing from table to table or poking or throwing things at others in an attempt to engage them in silliness. He created his biggest project pieces alone, usually by turning the video camera on himself in a quiet corner or in another room. Many of these pieces focused on school, which Charlie portrayed as a place with beloved teachers and treacherous peers.

Charlie Asserts Power Through Quiet Opposition

In one of his first blog entries, Charlie described the start of his school year (see Figure 3.2). He had just begun his first year of high school and reported to the group that he was struggling to adjust to the new setting. In this piece, Charlie detailed a few of the things he found hard about school, including navigating the space, keeping up with the academics, and the sheer number of people surrounding him. He described school as "hard, confusing, chaotic" and drew a direct correlation between that chaos at school and the tumult he felt internally. He also placed agency external to himself: *Summer* drained his memory, and *school* needed to calm down. School was not a place where Charlie saw himself as an agentive person.

Although Charlie found school to be fatiguing, he admired his teachers. He saw them as his allies and his best friends, and he created several pieces about them. When I asked the group once to describe their teachers, Charlie gushed, "Oh, they're perfect. I'm not being sarcastic, either.

Figure 3.2. Charlie's Blog Post About Adjusting to His First Year of High School

april 12

School is a chaotic and confusing maze of hallways and classrooms. Ok so, school this year has been hard, confusing, chaotic and don't even know what else... School is full of homework (which is hard). Confusing because summer drained my memory. Chaotic because there is close to 1,000 people in the buliding i'm in (there are 3, elementary, middle and high(i'm in high)). I hope school starts to calm down so i can too.

They're always cheerful, you can relate with them. . . . I told you I hang out with adults more than kids." In one of his autobiographical pieces, Charlie compared his science teacher to his favorite television character, describing him as "brilliant and amazing;" in another, he described his history teacher as "hysterically funny." Charlie was able to find other positive aspects of school; for example, he enjoyed working on the yearbook committee and often brought his yearbook with him to group.

Despite these bright reports on his teachers and activities, Charlie's other images of school were usually very dark. From everything he created in his work at the center, he showed that he experienced great difficulties socially. Being marginalized at school was a regular occurrence for many of the teens, and it became a frequent topic for the group. Once, after Elizabeth presented some of her pieces expressing marginalization in the school environment, Charlie also expressed feeling persecuted. I had opened the floor up to the group, asking if anyone else felt teased or bullied in school. Charlie volunteered the following:

Constantly. Never got any attention, though. I never stood up for myself. That's one thing I really try to stick to is not fighting back, cause my school has a strict policy. You'll instantly get detention and stuff. I've never hit anyone. I never got a detention. But the 9 years I've been in . . . of my life . . . I've always been constantly bullied and stuff.

Several of the teens nodded in agreement. Rory asked, "How?" and Charlie answered,

Any way imaginable. I've been punched, I've been kicked, I've been pressure pointed, I've been called names, I've been . . . everything imaginable. It's the worst possible scenario. To think, I'm so close to boiling over and I'm finally going to punch the people that bully me. I'm so close to that edge.

Trevor interrupted, "Didn't you tell the principal or the other teachers?" and Charlie replied:

I always tell or something. But I'm sick of being the tattletale. So I really still either . . . I do everything imaginable that people tell me . . . walk away, tattle on them—everything that every adult tells you to do with a normal bully. I've heard everything imaginable from all adults for 9 years. And nothing ever works.

There was a moment of silence in the group. "Why do you think kids bully you?" I asked. Charlie quickly responded, "I'm different. I'm a weak target. They can, basically."

Charlie's position of powerlessness in these pieces was a result of the bullying he experienced in school, and as a consequence, he did not seem to see himself as someone with personal agency in the school setting. Here, I am considering the concept of agency as Erstad and Silseth (2008) describe as "the capacity to make a difference linked to certain institutional and cultural practices" (p. 216). Charlie characterized himself as powerless to stop those who were tormenting him. He did begin, however, to describe himself as someone "on the edge," pushed to the point of retaliation. Even if he never actually acted as he said he might, I read this as a reframing of Charlie for himself. He began to describe himself as a person of authority, albeit limited and retaliatory, even if he chose not to exert this power. Throughout the year, Charlie characterized himself as someone who endured this vulnerability he felt at school.

In Charlie's dialogue with the other teens, he acknowledged the authoritative discourse of school, integrating it into his own talk about bullying. He said, "That's one thing I really try to stick to is not fighting back, 'cause my school has a strict policy." This code of conduct would not allow for Charlie to avenge himself, but it did not protect him from bullying either. One way to interpret this is as an *internally persuasive discourse* (Bakhtin, 1981). This internal conversation guided his behavior, and Charlie chose not to fight back against his oppressors. When Charlie said he wouldn't fight back because "You'll instantly get detention and stuff," he used this talk to legitimize his actions (or inaction). In the first turn, he described bullying but gave the consequences if he were to retaliate. In the second section, he provided more details about the nature of the abuse, drawing the listener closer to his view. He then revealed that he was working hard to restrain himself from fighting back. In the last turn, Charlie provided information on what he did instead of fighting back, which did not provide him with any relief. Throughout, he detailed abuses that might justify him defending himself. But he also justified his lack of action and his choice to endure the oppression.

I read Charlie as using his group project as a way to withstand the cruelty he suffered at school. He created pieces about bullying but always included some consideration of the rules that dictated his own behavior. Charlie garnered the support of the other teens throughout the year; some admired his strength to withstand, and others pushed him to act. Despite his threats to retaliate, Charlie continued to share stories of quiet opposition. He defined himself in his works by his ability to endure the ridicule he experienced at school, and I see his work as helping him to endure. I read the work he did in group as a way for Charlie to assert agency over his experiences. His narratives about these happenings informed his choices on when and how to act. His accounts also spoke to and with the accounts of others in the group who created their own renderings of oppressive experiences.

ELIZABETH: RESISTING OPPRESSION

Elizabeth's responses (Figure 3.3) to these three prompts are much like Charlie's—striking appraisals of her positionality. Notably, Elizabeth left her name off of this paper, writing "none" in the slot designated for her name. In this way, she started off by announcing her invisibility. In the first prompt, Elizabeth crossed out the word *look* and changed it to *feel* but then went on to provide a very physical (but negative) description of herself. She provided a critique of herself as "fat" and "ugly." She then described her self-image as "stupid," which she tied to the belief that no one likes her. Interestingly, Elizabeth did say that people try to help, but she admitted that did not improve her situation. She described herself as purposefully excluded and almost universally disliked. Elizabeth did provide one glimpse of respite from these harsh social experiences, provided by a friend at church; she valued both his advice and acceptance.[3] The tone of this piece was consistent with Elizabeth's manner in our group: She provided a harsh evaluation of herself and her circumstances, held a defensive stance, and was relatively confrontational.

Figure 3.3. Elizabeth's Response to Three Writing Prompts About How She Views Herself and How She Thinks Others View Her

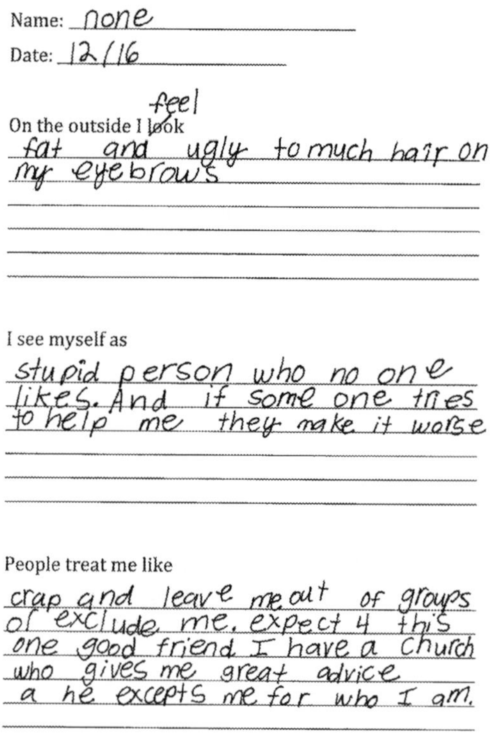

Name: _none_

Date: _12/16_

On the outside I ~~look~~ *feel*
fat and ugly to much hair on my eyebrows

I see myself as
stupid person who no one likes. And if some one tries to help me they make it worse

People treat me like
crap and leave me out of groups of exclude me. expect 4 this one good friend I have a church who gives me great advice a he excepts me for who I am.

Elizabeth's group attendance was sporadic. She attended the center infrequently, probably less than twice a month; she came to group even less often. Occasionally, she participated in the Teen Project several weeks in a row but then would be gone for a month or more before showing up again at the center. She was well liked within the group, though, and got along with several of the boys when she was there. Two of the teens had Elizabeth's cellphone number and would report on her when she was missing from group, relating that she had gone to her mom's house for a few weeks or had switched schools again. Once, Trevor told the group that he had called Elizabeth and they had gone to the movies together. Whenever Elizabeth was asked why she had missed group, she would say that she had been grounded, either for something she had done in school or for being disrespectful to her parents.

During the year in which this project took place, Elizabeth attended three different schools. She told the group she was "kicked out for bad behavior" at the first school, her local public high school. Elizabeth was then sent to another public high school in a neighboring urban district. She attended there less than a month before she left. I have never been sure if her parents took her out of that school or if she was expelled; Elizabeth reported both at various times. She was then tutored at home for a few weeks before she was enrolled in a state special education program on a campus for students with severe behavioral issues. Because of all these challenges, Elizabeth had a tense relationship with school and with teachers.

Despite her irregular attendance, Elizabeth participated in the group activities with enthusiasm and passion whenever she was present. She worked well with the other teens, provided complimentary feedback on others' projects, and remained engaged throughout the year. I never saw Elizabeth exhibit any problematic behaviors during group or at the center. Elizabeth's work at group sometimes addressed the problems she encountered at school. She openly talked with the other group members about her experiences, and she created several pieces describing events that led to her frequent school reassignments. Elizabeth retold the event that led to her attendance at the special education campus in an audio retelling a few weeks after it occurred:

My name is Elizabeth Westfall. One day at school, at lunchtime, this kid stood up and yelled my name very loudly: "Elizabeth Westfall is hot!" I was so embarrassed that I didn't know what to do. I had always gotten picked on since the 3rd grade. So I stood up and dumped chocolate milk all over the kid's head. I was called a "bully" the rest of the day. After dumping chocolate milk on the kid's head, I had to go down to the office and fill out a statement. My dad had to take me home because I was too embarrassed to ride home on the bus. When I got home, my mom found out what happened. A few days later, I told my mom that I wanted to go back to school to show kids that I'm not afraid, but she said, "No more school, you're getting tutored." Now, I have to go to this special program. But it's okay because I get along with guys better than girls,[4] and some things are worth getting in trouble for.

She also drew a comic strip of this same event (Figure 3.4). Elizabeth acknowledged that the event was not the only one that caused her to be removed from public education, but it was the final straw on an already precarious school situation for her. This event remained a major turning point in her year, and she worked it into her autobiography multiple times, through drawings, writing, and audio recordings.

Elizabeth Asserts Power by Fighting Back

Elizabeth encountered many distressing social situations in school, reporting almost constant teasing similar to Charlie's experiences. The two students, however, responded to their oppression in markedly different ways. Unlike Charlie's refusal to retaliate, Elizabeth fought back and told many stories of fighting back. In this particular story, Elizabeth detailed the teasing and bolstered her argument by providing the background that she had "gotten picked on since the 3rd grade."

Elizabeth also described her motivation for her actions, not that she was angry, but that she was embarrassed. She described being unsure of what to do. Ultimately, Elizabeth decided to reposition herself so she was not the

Figure 3.4. Elizabeth's Comic Strip Retelling the Event that Led to Her Attendance at a Special Education Campus

victim. In this story about bullying, Elizabeth turned the table and became the bully herself.

In many of Elizabeth's stories, her claims for power in school often got her in trouble. In her narratives, she frequented the principal's office and detention. She had difficulty maintaining relationships with others at school, perhaps because she was seen as an outcast and perhaps because she didn't remain in one place long enough to build lasting friendships. Despite what seemed to be almost constant punishment, Elizabeth often spoke of her actions as she did in this case, as "worth getting in trouble for."

Elizabeth told this particular story of pouring milk over a classmate and its consequences on four separate occasions at group. Her telling and retelling of this event may have been cathartic for her, helping to integrate an unsettling event into her self-understanding (Hull & Katz, 2006). Liz used her work in the Teen Project to explore her problematic experiences of school. Whereas Charlie told stories of endurance, Liz told stories of resistance. She may not have seen herself in a position of power at school, but she would not allow herself to silently withstand persecution.

This almost-constant stance of resistance and protectionism was exhausting. Elizabeth usually arrived at group with her guard up, tense from a long day at school. It would take her a few minutes to begin to ease up, and her release of that tension was often visible. Even on a small scale, when social issues were personal and not situated at school, Elizabeth showed determination to fight back. For example, during one group session, Elizabeth shared a series of texts she had saved from an exchange with another girl, Cassy, whom she knew from school (see Figure 3.5). Elizabeth described this exchange one afternoon to the group and photographed the texts as artifacts for her project. The exchange began when Cassy, one of Liz's classmates, sent her a picture text. Elizabeth did not show the text but described it only as "inappropriate" and "bullying." Elizabeth demanded that these types of images not be sent to her, adding, "I got an idea I wnt talk to u at all." Through text, Elizabeth defended herself, telling Cassy it was hard for her to make friends and calling her a backstabber like everyone else. In these texts, Elizabeth struggled to regain control of a social situation that had deteriorated. She asserted herself, highlighting the strength of her tone with capital letters. Yet in the last text, she made herself vulnerable by admitting she had a hard time making friends.

Elizabeth tried to assert power over her own circumstances in this text exchange in the same way she did with her experiences at school. She kept up an almost constant defense, prepared to fight back in all cases. In these works that Liz created in group, she portrayed herself as someone clamoring for agency. She spoke up loudly and often, and she told stories of how she stood up for herself at school. She authored herself as a young woman fighting for strength and control over her own circumstances.

Despite her irregular attendance, Elizabeth formed strong connections with some of the other teens. In the context of the group, I think we all saw

Figure 3.5. Elizabeth's Text Messages Illustrating Power and Vulnerability

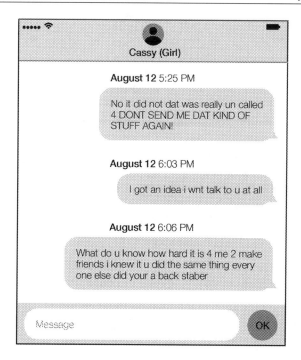

her as a powerful person, a tough girl who wouldn't stand for any abuse. But she also showed her vulnerability in her interactions and her work. I read Elizabeth as a young woman learning to assert herself and learning all the social negotiations that go along with it. Through her connections with others in the group, she had the courage to position herself vis-à-vis school, meeting some very distressing issues head-on. This writing and creating and positioning and interpreting was an agentive act for Elizabeth. She learned about herself through and with the other teens and drew power from those connections. This youth, who was considered so problematic in school that she could not be served in a general education program, participated in complex literacy and social practices in the after-school group. She created powerful works, like her audio story and her comic strip, and she did so with a verve that demonstrated real engagement. She collaborated with others around this work, sharing her writing, incorporating feedback from the other group members, and talking back to their works as well. This is remarkably compelling from a student who was dismissed by more than one school system. Given the space for this kind of work, Elizabeth was insightful, generous with her thoughts, and self-reflective. Given the assumptions about students like Elizabeth, these opportunities are critical. This work shows significant potential for the voices of marginalized students to be heard.

CODY: REFRAMING OPPRESSION

Situating Cody Within the Group

Cody's responses to the writing prompts (Figure 3.6) were short but poignant. Like Elizabeth, he crossed out the word *look* and replaced it with *feel*, but Cody's response was much more positive, describing himself as a caring person. Indeed, Cody showed a great deal of empathy in a variety of ways. For example, in the vignette that begins this chapter, Cody was the one who recognized that Elizabeth was upset and called the group's attention to this. In the third response, Cody echoed his earlier sentiments about school, writing that he was treated like "a retarded hobo." Although he never explained what he meant by that term, the negative stigmas attached to both words lead to the conclusion that Cody did not feel respected by others.

Figure 3.6. Cody's Response to Three Writing Prompts About How He Views Himself and How He Thinks Others View Him

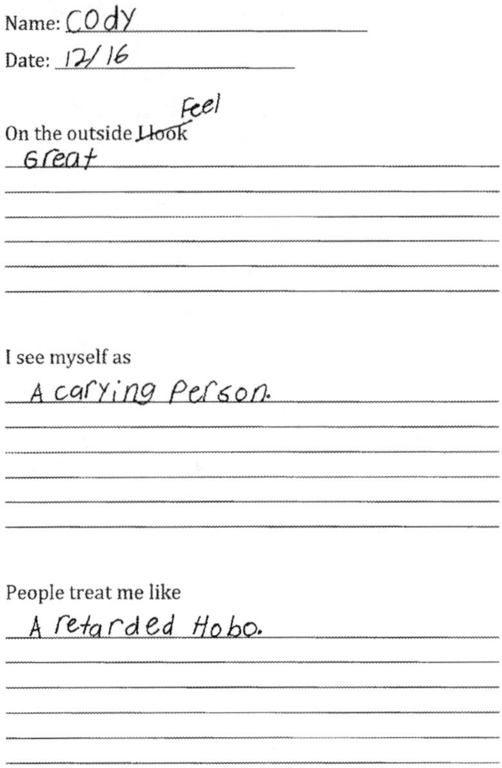

Name: Cody

Date: 12/16

On the outside ~~I look~~ Feel
Great

I see myself as
A carying person.

People treat me like
A retarded Hobo.

Cody was our group's most prolific creator. He kept a blog and posted at least weekly and sometimes daily. He drew comics, created stop-motion animation, and videotaped himself brushing his teeth. He photographed his family. He described minute details of his room in one lengthy audio recording. He wrote poetry, painted, and created elaborate collages. Despite this abundance of material, it was difficult to get to know Cody through his work. Cody's stories changed, and they changed frequently. Cody might write in a blog post that his grandfather was sick, then he would come to group and say he had come from his grandfather's funeral. Everyone would offer condolences, only to see Cody's grandfather, alive and well, pick him up from the center at the group's end. Cody told stories of his three-legged dog, of his cousin who lived in his basement, of his after-school job picking vegetables with migrant workers. Some of his stories were true, some were not, but they were all elaborately inconsistent and difficult to believe.

One thing I did know was that Cody experienced much of the social isolation at school that the other teens underwent. Cody joined our group as a referral from his school. His special education teacher, concerned for Cody's self-esteem, had called the center to inquire about resources for Cody and his family. She described Cody as withdrawn, quiet, and tense. The Cody I met in group was none of these things. In fact, I would describe him as boisterous and fanciful. He got along well with the other teens and often plotted witty schemes and suggested silly activities. When we brainstormed ways to tell a story, Cody's suggestions included telling stories in Morse code, training a parrot, and burping out the stories. In one video, he made a hat out of a potted plant and marched it around on Elizabeth's head, all the while singing "Miss America" as loudly as possible.

Cody Asserts Power by Altering His Stories

Cody sometimes focused on school as a topic for his project, and his stories about school were as varied as the rest of his works. Often, he addressed difficulties he had at school. In one blog entry (Figure 3.7), Cody wrote about how homework affected his grades. In another work, Cody and Charlie made a video in which the boys interviewed each other about school. While Cody stretched out on a couch in the therapy room, Charlie videotaped and asked questions from behind the camera:

Charlie: What is your day like?
Cody: My day is horrible. Every day I get picked on. I have to have a stinkin' teacher walk me around the school just so I don't get picked on all day.
Charlie: How do others make you feel?
Cody: Others make me feel horrible. Why do you think I have that teacher?

Figure 3.7. Cody's Blog Post About How Homework Affected His Grades

> **april 1**
>
> Sometimes I have trouble in school with handing in my home work. Sometimes I just forget to do it or I forget it at home. Other times I just do not bother to do it. Then it affects how my grades come out to be. In the end I end up with lower grades then I wanted.

In these two pieces, Cody portrayed himself as someone who has both academic and social difficulty in school. But at other times, he denied that this was the case. Once, when Cody stayed after group to work on his project, I tried engaging him in a conversation about school. I wanted to get more information about the experiences he had related in his blog and videos. Cody was very hesitant and he gave me only short answers, some that directly contradicted the work he had done in group:

Beth: Do you like school?
Cody: It's okay.
Beth: Do you ever get bullied?
Cody: No, not really.
Beth: Huh. Did you ever get bullied before?
Cody: No, not really.
Beth: Hmmm. Who are your friends?
Cody: I can't recall their names.
Beth: Oh. Well, what are your teachers like?
Cody: Most of them are okay.
Beth: Do they know you have autism?
Cody: I don't know.
Beth: How do you do in school?
Cody: Good.
Beth: Who's the best teacher in the school, do you think?
Cody: Miss Russell.
Beth: Why?
Cody: She's hot.
Beth: Oh. [pause] Do you ever get in trouble at school?
Cody: No.
Beth: Did you used to get in trouble at school?
Cody: A little. I don't want to talk about that.

Cody was posturing here, perhaps because this questioning was on my terms and not his. He and I are fairly close and usually have a good rapport. In fact, Cody once invited me to his school to give a presentation on autism to his class. He even volunteered to appear on the local news to talk about autism and promote a fundraising event at the center. But in this piece, I'm asking Cody successive questions and he's deflecting them as quickly as possible, giving me only short, terse answers. At one point, he seems to be intentionally provocative, calling his teacher "hot." The most information he provided was in the last turn when he admitted that he had been in trouble at school but that he didn't want to talk about it. It was clear from the beginning that he was not interested in deep revelations at this time, but I persisted. He pushed me off in several ways until I finally relented. Cody exercised social power in this piece and in the group. He chose when and how to represent himself through his stories. Narratives are, as Hull and Katz (2006) describe, dynamic; they depend on the relationship between the narrator and the audience. As they explain, "How we represent ourselves in storied worlds depends on who we are trying to be in relation to others in the present" (p. 45). Cody created deliberate portraits of himself that were particular to his audience, the space in which the story was told, and the story he wanted to tell. This is a sophisticated use of narrative, and one that might not be expected of a student like Cody based on his diagnosis. He was able to make keen assessments about himself, his audience, and particular situations, all while maintaining a strong narrative voice. These changing narratives were one way that Cody claimed agency over his circumstances.

Cody may have also tried to assert power over his educational history by altering the stories he told about his experiences. In one video, Cody recorded a story about school:

Once I was so mad . . . at, at a teacher . . .
I picked up a chair, I threw it across the room.
Slammed it onto her desk as she was doing her work!
'Cause I waited a while, until she went back to doing whatever, and I didn't get in trouble,
and I was wicked mad at her though. So I threw it . . . she, I, I knock her out. Then the assistant comes after me.
And I just throw my desk right at her, she trips over it, she falls to the ground. And I'm like,
Storm the school! Wooh! And all the kids came with me stormin' the school.
I had the cops on me in, in no time.
For some reason I got charged with sexual assault. [laughs]
Probably because I ripped the teacher's shirt off. But I wasn't charged for attempted murder.
I had to go to court, though.
I was like 6 years old, and I was sitting in court! [laughs] Being sued! [laughs]
[baby voice] But I didn't do it! The teacher made me mad.

When I first viewed this video of Cody's story, I set it aside as unusable for this project. I knew the story was not true, and I felt any audience would see the same. I thought a story this fanciful would bring into question the authenticity of anything Cody wrote, and I was concerned it would jeopardize the validity of my work. I kept returning to this story, however, wondering how it contributed to the picture that Cody created of himself. Drawing on Riessman's (2008) functions of narrative, I began to see this story as a *situated truth*, created with purpose for Cody.

Riessman (2008) lists several functions of narrative: "Individuals use the narrative form to remember, argue, justify, persuade, engage, entertain, and even mislead an audience" (p. 8). I would argue that Cody is utilizing many of these functions in this piece. He *remembers* an incident, probably in its true form, and reframes it for his audience. Cody uses rhetorical skills to *persuade* the audience that this is how it really happened. We become engaged in Cody's experience. It is simultaneously *entertaining* and *argumentative*. Cody took control of his narrative and turned it on its head.

Cody's story also holds many of the linguistic features of a performance drama (Riessman, 2008); it contains direct speech, asides, repetition, expressive sounds, and changing verb tense. These conventions all have a function in Cody's story, and he used them purposefully in his work. Direct speech is often used to engage the audience, which Cody did with his own words both halfway through and at the end, as well as to increase credibility. There are clearly some pieces that defy logic. Cody resolved these inconsistencies with the use of explanatory asides. Cody also marked important moments through repetition, such as his restating that he threw the chair. Expressive sounds like "wooh" and the infantile voice mark both turning points and resolution. Cody also utilized verb tense in an interesting way, alternating the past tense with the historical present. As Riessman (2008) explains, "Switching tenses underscores the agency of the narrator" (p. 113). In this way, Cody moved himself from passive to active, affording himself greater power over the situation. Cody portrayed himself as a person of great strength, even at a young age.

In this piece, Cody repositioned himself as someone who had the power and strength to fight authority, even as someone who had the influence to lead others in a revolt against an institution. He constructed himself as a critic of the interplay of power at school. For Cody, autobiography became performance as he created different versions of himself. In this context, I consider Kaare and Lundby's (2008) claim that authenticity in digital storytelling is not a straightforward notion; the idea of "being yourself" assumes that there is one self to represent. It reduces the multiplicity of identity. In interrogating the truth about Cody's stories, we find that there is no singular Cody; he and all of the teens represented multiple selves throughout the year.

MAKING SPACE FOR INQUIRY

Charlie, Elizabeth, Cody, and the other students in the group all shared common experiences of school—experiences of being marginalized, moments of struggle, and difficulty making space for themselves in school. They all brought stories of oppression in some form from school with them to group. I knew that they all had stories to share, that their lives were not, as Smith's (1996) article had characterized, *unautobiographical*. One of the most compelling products of this work is that we are invited to see how students experience school from their own perspectives, not from data in their progress reports or measureable objectives in their IEPs. The intimacy of their stories provides an insider view of an experience that is fraught with assumptions. This group grew as a setting for critical action research as the teens made space in this after-school program to build their own inquiry community (Cochran-Smith & Lytle, 2009).

We may not have known that this transformative work would take place, but it was not exactly unintentional. This group was set up in a way that made it possible for the students to assume a more agentive stance about their own lives and circumstances (Hull, 2003). In several studies of students engaged in digital media (Bauman & Briggs, 1990; Hull & Katz, 2006), the authors propose four features as central to agentive work:

1. Access
2. Legitimacy
3. Competence
4. Values

They define *access* as being allowed to enter the structures and engage in practices that produce this kind of work. In our group, the students were given a space for this work and access to tools, activities, and a group of peers. By *legitimacy*, they mean that they are given the authority to create. The teens in the program were legitimized in this work and positioned as authorities on their own lives. The authors define *competence* as being considered capable of doing the work. Drawing on Biklen's (2005) discussions about the presumption of competence for individuals with autism, I presumed that all of the youth were competent in their ability to self-represent, and they demonstrated their competence throughout. The final feature proposed as central to agentive work is *values*, or that the work is considered valuable by others. Our group shared the understanding that their creations would be considered productive contributions to the work we were doing as a group.

The structure of the group provided activities, materials, and opportunities for this type of work. The group members themselves solidified the relationships that made this work productive. This group became an embodiment of the idea that individuals, "banded together in communities of practice, can author . . . new selves and new cultural worlds" (Holland & Lachicotte, 2007, p. 116). The work of the group was a contagion and the interactions between the teens in and around the works further built each piece. The students considered the experiences of the others in the group and learned to integrate others' experiences into their own. Their voices merged, and pulled apart, and influenced others' stories.

The data from the students' explorations of their experiences in and out of school showed how these teens, like the cases in Hull and Katz's (2006) study, not only learned how to compose multimedia narratives, but how to construct viable images of themselves. As Hull and Katz (2006) explain, development of self-understanding can be entwined with the creation of multimedia works. The students used these works to author themselves as competent. They created social worlds in which they were in charge, in which they made decisions about when and how to act/react. They constructed their own authority by creating multimodal works about their life experiences, and particularly about moments when they encountered oppression. With one another, the teens learned to endure, and to resist, and to reframe their experiences.

As these students positioned themselves vis-à-vis school, they opened themselves up to collaboration. The forming of an inquiry community was accomplished by the contagion effect of sharing common experiences, showing empathy, and creating images of those experiences together. All of this was done among a group of kids who are not expected, based on their diagnoses, to engage in this kind of work. The context of the Teen Project is what enabled this work to transpire. Although these three cases illustrated three different responses to oppression at school, the results were more complex than that. In responding to oppression and sharing those responses with one another, the group became an inquiry community and *collectively* claimed agency over their own experiences. As we will see in the next chapter, this inquiry community also became central in the students' explorations of autism and their own labels.

CHAPTER 4

"Nobody's normal in a way"

Writing Ourselves into the Story of Autism

> What's it like to have autism? I can't really tell you because I don't know
> what it's like to be another person—like a normal person. Actually, nobody's
> normal in a way.
>
> —Cody, peer video interview

One of my primary questions entering into this work centered on how autistic youth understand and question autism. Going into this work with a view of autism as socially constructed (Biklen, 2005; Kliewer & Biklen, 2001; Kluth, 2003), I was interested in seeing how the teens, as individuals with that label, built understandings of autism. I was also interested in how they took up this topic, not just as individuals but together as an inquiry community (Cochran-Smith & Lytle, 2009). I expected that they would influence one another's ideas about autism, and that their understandings of that diagnosis would be affected by our interactions around the label of autism. Throughout this chapter, we see how these explorations built the youth's understandings of themselves and their label. They questioned what it means to be "normal" and used their narrative works to disrupt the traditional stigma of disability.

(DE)CONSTRUCTING AUTISM

The topic of autism was rarely foregrounded in the teens' works, but it hung around the periphery of everything they did. This was, after all, a group held at an autism center for teens who were labeled autistic. Autism was an inescapable notion in our work, even by default. It did seem, however, that each of the teens had a different understanding of autism and a different relationship to its implications. Some came to group knowing a lot about their label and how they got it; for others, it was a relatively new concept. Often, they discussed autism incidentally and seemed to construct and reconstruct their ideas about autism with one another.

During one group meeting early in the year, I asked the students what they knew about autism. Billy was the first to speak up, offering, "Autism is that sometimes you can be born with it. Your parents know about it. And they find out you have it. You do something." Cody, who was sitting next to Billy, had been fiddling with his cellphone. At Billy's comment, Cody put the phone down and added, "It has something to do with the brain's connections and the nervous system. I don't know. It's not visible, exactly." Then Trevor joined in, saying, "All I know is I have one of the forms." Several of the teens nodded, and a few said, "Yeah" or "Me, too." Elizabeth, in her usual direct manner, asked Trevor, "So is that, are you scared of that or are you just okay with it?" Trevor replied, "I'm fine with it. It hasn't changed my life, like at all." Elizabeth persisted: "But how do you know if it's changed your life if you don't know what life would be like without it?" This seemed to be an interesting idea for the group. When Trevor exclaimed, "I don't know!" several of the teens agreed, saying, "Yeah, right?" or "Whoa." Trevor went on but stumbled through his words this time:

Hmmm, I don't know. It's hard to explain. I don't know how to explain it. You would say it's, it just makes you [pause] who you are? I don't know how to explain it. I just don't know how to explain it.

Cody offered his own insights. He said, "It's more near to being an average person than, say, like someone who can't talk. They have trouble learning." Billy added, "They sometimes focus on one subject. If they focus on one subject, that is the subject they are going to major in, for the rest of their life. They don't know what to say. They don't focus." There was a pause in the conversation, and then Charlie slowly offered his thoughts:

I know autism is like a scale, and it makes us different from other people. It doesn't really make me feel different. I guess [pause] that it just means that I learn slower. Make more mistakes than other people, I guess.

In this discussion, the teens struggled to construct a definition of autism that worked for all of them. Billy defined autism as something one is born with, an idea that I heard the teens use on more than one occasion to assert that autism was not contagious. Billy also defined autism as something that "parents know about" and then can discover in their children. When Cody entered into the conversation of the group, he first interjected with a more scientific definition of autism, alluding to the neurological system. Later, he set up autism as a range, with an "average person" on one end and "someone who can't talk" on the other. He seemed to see himself and the other group members somewhere between those two poles but closer to average than not.[1] This talk about autism reflects the dominant discourse about autism. The teens were already taking up a positivist stance, one that defines autism as something internal or neurological. Both Cody and Charlie reflected the predominant language around autism as a "spectrum" disorder, a common conception about autism. Several times, the teens defined autism in a negative sense, such as causing a lack of focus, increased mistakes, and slow learning.

The teens' struggle to define autism is not uncommon, especially considering that even the medical definition of autism is a complicated one involving multiple checklists and subjective notions (Biklen, 2005; Kluth, 2003). Despite the dominance of the medical model, alternative understandings of autism are beginning to emerge. For disability studies theorists, autism, like other disabilities, is not something objective but rather socially constructed (Kliewer & Biklen, 2001; Molloy & Vasil, 2004).

The social model of disability positions autism as a product of the social practices and policies that surround it. In our group discussion, Cody described autism as being "not visible." For some individuals, autism can be considered an "invisible culture," one that is not always recognized by others. As Erickson (2010) explains:

> Differences in invisible culture can be troublesome in circumstances of intergroup conflict. The difficulty lies in our inability to recognize others' differences in ways of acting as cultural rather than personal. We tend to naturalize other people's behaviors and blame them—attributing intentions, judging competence—without realizing that we are experiencing culture rather than nature. (p. 39)

Critical disability theory views autism as socially situated, not an absolute category. This view is at odds with the more traditional positivist models that consider disability as isolated to an individual and not mediated by society (Kliewer & Biklen, 2001; Molloy & Vasil, 2004). Both Cody and Billy described autism as an abnormality here, something to be recognized and neurologically attributed. They also described autism from a distance in this conversation, not yet revealing their own personal experiences with such a label.

Trevor changed the conversation to put it on a more personal level by applying the label of autism to himself. An interesting exchange occurred between Trevor and Elizabeth, in which Elizabeth asked Trevor's feelings on being labeled. She only gave him two choices, however: to be okay with the label or to be scared. If the question had been more open-ended, Trevor might have responded differently. Given only the two options, he said that he was fine with it. He even elaborated that it hadn't changed his life. This led Elizabeth to make an insightful point: Trevor, and all of the group members, cannot know what life would be like without autism. This caused Trevor to try to clarify, but left him struggling with his explanation.

This idea seemed to strike everyone but Elizabeth and Cody as a novel concept, and it became a thread that continued through many other discussions. By troubling this notion, the youth began to engage in a theoretical conversation that would continue throughout the year. As I will show, their understandings of autism were predicated upon how autism played out in their individual lives. This was a very personal examination, one that could not be considered separately from their understandings of themselves.

In the aforementioned group discussion, Billy later went on to talk about focus, which he seemed to position as both a positive and a negative trait. He may have been commenting on verbal ability as well when he said, "They don't know what to say." Even in this exchange, Billy did not claim autism as an identity for himself. Charlie, however, did speak from the first-person perspective, saying, "It makes us different from other people." Charlie said that he didn't feel different from other kids, but he did name himself as learning at a slow pace and making more errors than others.

This was our first foray as a group into constructing our own understandings of autism with one another. Throughout the year, this discussion about defining autism would resurface in many ways. Often, it involved one or more group members struggling to explain autism to others in the group. For example, Charlie struggled to establish what autism meant for his own abilities. He sometimes described what he found difficult, such as understanding or concentrating, as a trait of autism. He once defined autism in this way:

It means you have a hard time concentrating. I can concentrate when I'm alone and stuff but not at things like school and stuff when they really want you to. 'Cause I, I concentrate when I want to, not when they make me or they want me to. I concentrate on my own time, not when they want me to.

It was sometimes difficult for the teens to define autism in favorable terms. The definition was often focused on the negative, such as what they could not do or what was difficult for them. Charlie even seemed to explain autism as an inability to perform on demand, saying that he could only concentrate when he wanted to.

In another case, Carson discussed how he saw autism as causing him to struggle socially, not because of how others viewed him, but because his "social problems make it hard to know who is a friend." Carson explained further: "Huh, well, I used to let people just go to be, you know, accept them as friends, now it's coming to the attention that they would have to be nice to me for a long time that determines whether they're a friend or not." Carson attributed something he found difficult (understanding friendship) to his diagnosis of autism. He discussed autism as a cause of social difficulties because of these misunderstandings.

The teens did not always agree with one another as they created these notions of autism. Sometimes I found their explanations so problematic that I could not refrain from adding to or correcting their understandings, despite my intentions to allow the students to work out these understandings together. For example, Charlie once mentioned that he had heart surgery as a baby and suggested that it caused his autism. Billy, who also happened to have had heart surgery as a youth, connected with this idea. This was one of the few times I found myself asserting clinical understandings about autism to the youth, telling the boys that autism was not caused by heart surgery. Despite my hesitation to define autism for the students, none of them questioned why I provided such a definitive meaning at this time. After I spoke, Cody added, "Yeah, no one knows what causes autism." Afraid the teens would continue with this idea, I interjected again, saying, "But they know it is *not* caused by heart surgery." Billy seemed to accept this and never mentioned it again, but Charlie sometimes returned to the notion that his heart surgery was a catalyst for his autism diagnosis.

All of these constructions of autism situated it as something internal, manifesting as a set of behaviors or understandings. Often, I heard the language of the dominant discourse in the youth's explanations, as information they gleaned from parents, teachers, doctors, media, or situations in which they heard autism discussed. None of the youth expressed a very clear or simple definition of autism, but explained it by how the diagnosis affected their individual lives.

INTERROGATING "NORMAL"

In discussions throughout the year, the students frequently used terms such as *normal* and *different*. It was clear that the group could not discuss autism without engaging in the dominant discourse, one that set them as "abnormal" or "other." As with the social construction of autism, I am considering the notion of "normal" as situated as well. Campano and Simon (2010) describe the ideology of normal as "a deeply ingrained social and material practice that permeates almost every aspect of education and is manifested in a web of interrelated pedagogical policies, practices, and structures" (p. 222). *Normal* and *abnormal* are created, mediated, and maintained by practice and policy.

As a group, we wrestled with the construction of normal and what it meant to us. Cody, for example, continually insisted that "nobody is normal," a theme that surfaced often. After this idea came up more than once, I posed this question to the group: Who gets to decide what is normal? I told them that I heard them discussing the word *normal* often, and I thought this could be a question we should start to think about. I wrote the question on a piece of paper and hung it on the side wall of our main meeting room. I noticed that the teens began to avoid the word *normal* itself, but its meaning continued to creep into our conversations and our work. For example, many of the teens began to substitute the word *different* for the term *abnormal*. There did not seem to be a way to avoid the dominant discourse around disability.

The best we could do was to think critically about what *normal* meant in a social context. Often, this consisted of one or more of the teens using some iteration of the word *normal*, followed by my asking for clarification of what they meant by that term. Occasionally, the students would ask one another, or one would refer to the question on the wall. Other times, Cody or another student would take us back to the idea that "nobody is normal."

Sometimes the teens described themselves and their own traits in terms of how *normal* they were. For example, Carson recorded a video of himself in which he discussed that others made fun of him for what they considered an abnormal behavior. Carson said, "Sometimes I talk with my eyes closed. And what's the big deal with that? Everybody does it." He seemed to want to position that particular behavior he exhibited as normal, or something that everyone did. Despite naming this behavior as something he was teased about, Carson wanted to view it as typical. He attributed many other traits to autism, like his anxiety, his inability to tie his shoes, or his difficulties keeping friends. This particular behavior, closing his eyes while talking, Carson insisted was "normal."

At other times, the youth considered being different as a positive trait. In one video, Charlie explained, "Well, I guess you could call it different, but I'm still a kid. I can think for myself, which is different. I'm not a bully, I don't bully anyone, which is different from most people." Charlie positioned his differences in this way as *better* than his peers. He felt that other teens were bullies and succumbed easily to peer pressure. He saw his own difficulties following social cues to be a positive thing because he thought for himself and did not mistreat others.

The students even described their differences on a scale of negative and positive. Sometimes they argued that their differences were not *as bad* as other traits. Charlie, for example, explained autism in the following way:

It means that you might have a harder time understanding. But you're not stupid. You're not, like, what Hitler thinks of people. You're different, you're not wrong. You're just different. It doesn't mean anything.

Here, Charlie positioned *stupid* and *wrong* as being less favorable than autistic. During another group session, I asked Trevor what he would want people to know about autism. He responded, "It doesn't make you stupid; it doesn't make you retarded. It just means you're different."

As a strict number on a scale, some of these kids are, in fact, labeled with an intellectual disability in their evaluation reports; some of the older reports do use the term *mentally retarded* as a clinical label. Yet the teens understand *retarded* to be a very negative label, even more disadvantageous than autism. They had reconciled themselves as being different, but did not want to be considered *stupid* or *retarded*. In this way, the youth engaged in a ranking of self-worth. The notion of *normal* always involves power and the distribution of social capital (Campano & Simon, 2010; Gee, 1996). These students are not only labeled as *abnormal* or *different*, but through this labeling are positioned as inherently less valuable, less powerful, and more socially dispensable than their peers.[2]

EXPLORING THE POTENTIAL OF NARRATIVE WORKS

Many disability rights groups have taken up the motto "Nothing about us without us," which is to argue that those with disability should be involved in the creation of policies about disability (Franits, 2005). Individual inclusion, highlighted by the use of personal stories of disability, has come to the forefront of disability studies. Narratives have been used by the disability community to affirm identity and assert basic rights (Engel & Munger, 2007). Individuals with disability labels recounting their own stories have the potential to push against the current discourse on disability. In fact, the contribution of these counternarratives has been a goal of disability studies (Barton, 2007). Narrative can help overcome barriers for those with disability by positioning them in power over their own stories.

The crafting of one's own story, even within the constraints of the dominant discourse, allows an individual authorship of her or his own experiences. Wilson and Lewiecki-Wilson (2001) further explain the purpose of many disability narratives as follows:

> If marginalization is in part a function of discourse that excludes and/or objectifies, autobiography has considerable potential to counter stigmatizing or patronizing portrayals of disability because it is a medium in which disabled people may have a high degree of control over their own images. (p. 78)

Personal narratives provide an outlet for those silenced by marginalization, drawing them into positions of authority and power over their own stories.

Public narratives hold a particularly prominent place in disability literature, especially as related to this work. Thomas (1999) defines public narratives as "those narratives attached to cultural and institutional formations larger than the single individual" (p. 62). Disability narratives are always influenced by societal definitions of ability and disability and can be considered public narratives because of these underlying assumptions. Counternarratives often present the social barriers to basic rights that individuals with disability experience. Personal narrative can serve to powerfully reframe our understandings of disability (Gill, 2004).

DISRUPTING THE AUTISM NARRATIVE

When the students were given a chance to write their histories, autism was rarely addressed head-on. Instead, the youth explored aspects of their lives that could be related to their diagnosis. This is demonstrated, for example, in a comic strip drawn by Billy (Figure 4.1). Billy drew the first frame with only the setting, a grassy field on a sunny day. In the second frame, we see a flower centered on the grass. Next, Billy drew two people, labeled "me" and "Sam," with a heart between the two. In the subsequent frames, Billy drew himself picking the flower and presenting it to Sam. In the final frame, the two characters appear to embrace or kiss. This comic shows Billy as a young man hoping for social connection, not one controlled by the self-isolation associated with autism. This is consistent throughout the collective works presented in this book. These works focused on the connections of family, the security and insecurity of home, and the social difficulties faced at school. Given the opportunity to name and describe themselves, none of the students wrote "autistic" as a primary label for themselves. When individuals with autism get to label themselves, they get to decide which interpretations to privilege (Biklen, 2005).

Figure 4.1. Billy's Comic Strip Depicting Billy as a Young Man Hoping for Social Connection

As the teens began to craft their own histories, disrupting the autism narrative took on some urgency. Some of the group members saw this work as a chance to respond to the names they were accustomed to hearing. For example, Charlie created a video in which he explained that others have low expectations for him, calling him "fat" and "different." Charlie, however, saw himself as much more capable than people expected. Charlie increasingly created pieces about his capabilities, even as he related the oppression he was experiencing. These works seemed to be a way for Charlie to talk back to his oppressors, even if he never shared his work outside of our group.

Describing themselves and their own experiences can be a powerful way to counter the stereotypical images of autism. As Goodman (2003) found in his own research with youth and digital literacies, "Not only does it matter how teenagers are named, it matters who does the naming" (p. 30). In our group, the students offered pictures of themselves that were outside the dominant frame of isolation and deficiency. If known more widely, their work could act as a counternarrative to perceptions of autistic youth as unsocial and incapable.

MANAGING A STIGMATIZED IDENTITY

Disclosing a diagnosis of disability has become one area of discussion in disability studies. Some individuals labeled with a disability, particularly in the case of physical disability, may not always have a choice; their label may be a part of their physical appearance. For some autistics, self-disclosure is a choice. Because it is largely, as Cody noted, an invisible disability, sometimes people with autism can choose not to tell others they are autistic. Some in the autistic community, however, find autism such an integral part of their identity that they could not hide it. A third group contends that autism should be a point of pride, a way to reclaim power over the diagnosis (Shore, 2004). In Biklen's (2005) discussion of the autobiographical writings of Blackman (2001), an autistic adult, he explains that she sees disclosure as necessary for her own well-being. She desires acknowledgment and accommodation, things that cannot be properly provided to her without acknowledging her differences. Others, then, see the disclosure of diagnosis as a means to an end: the only way to access the services and accommodations they need to be successful (Biklen, 2005).

The teens, like the broader autistic community, had differing views on the benefits and drawbacks of self-disclosure. Some, like Ivan, saw their autism diagnosis as private and inconsequential to others. He explained to the group, "Me? Nobody really knows about [my autism diagnosis]. Just me and my mom. My family, nobody knows that I have it. I don't feel like it's important to tell anyone. Nobody will care." Others worried about the social consequences of disclosing their diagnoses. Billy discussed this when relating a story about a pizza shop owner who asked if he was autistic:

He asked if I had autism. People with autism, we don't like being pointed out to the whole world. When I told my dad about it, he also found it offensive. Because autism isn't something to be proud of. Some people with autism don't focus on what they are saying, don't focus on what they are doing. If you tell someone you have autism, that can hurt. It's better to just not tell anyone you have autism. I would recommend that people don't mention having autism, until they are asked. But if their friends want to know, don't tell them. Try, they'll try telling everyone at school. Then you'll be the one that no one likes.

This was not an uncommon sentiment. Given the bullying and marginalization the teens experienced in school and the overarching stigma of disability, they felt the need to protect themselves.

Within the group, however, the teens were often more open about being labeled. In the safer space where the label was what they all had in common, even the students who had never disclosed their diagnosis to anyone did so in group. Billy, who had just recommended that others keep autism private, posted several pictures to his blog about autism or disability, including a picture of him holding a T-shirt from an autism walk and a picture of the disability tag on his family car. Even Ivan, who said that only his mom knew his diagnosis, spoke openly about being autistic during group interactions.

Others struggled with disclosing and hiding their label. Carson was one student who discussed this. He described the prejudices that came along with his label, but he also craved the chance to provide an explanation to his peers. Carson created an audio recording in which he discussed this idea:

Does the phrase *stereotyping* come into mind when it comes to middle school
    and high school?
Sometimes it does. It's easily noticed. They just think I'm annoying.
Well, they don't quite get it.
Unless I explain what I'm trying to tell them.
Which they won't let me
How am I ever going to tell them
That I don't really mean to be annoying and I'm just trying to explain
    something?
Now that's a tough one.

On the one hand, Carson felt he would be stereotyped if others knew he was autistic. On the other hand, he was already ostracized and disclosure might help him explain himself. He wanted to share but was afraid to do so.

Others recognized the patronizing that sometimes accompanies a diagnosis. Charlie, who was so ostracized in school, disclosed his autism to peers at both church and a local community center. In these places, he explained, kids were nicer to him than at school. He wasn't bullied in the same way as school, but he was treated differently from the other kids, sometimes, as he explained in a group discussion, in a way that made him feel uncomfortable:

Ehh, ASD just makes you who you are. You have it, you can't get rid of it. It doesn't mean it's gonna kill you or anything. It just means that, you're just different. And I get treated differently. Sometimes you get treated in a nice way. Like they treat you better, because, either they know what you're going through, which isn't really anything, or, or, they feel bad for you, which they shouldn't, but they do because . . . [trails off]

Charlie experienced both sides of the disclosure dilemma. He was bullied at school but sometimes patronized at church. He felt others looked down on him in both scenarios.

There was also the stigma of autism as a disability to contend with. The teens often expressed frustration at being combined in a category with other disabilities. Many of them were in special education classrooms with other children not diagnosed with autism but with a variety of other labels. In one group interaction, Charlie tried to distinguish autism as something more positive (or less disabled) than another diagnosis:

Autism doesn't make you mean; it makes you not understand. Well, I might have autism, but at least it doesn't make you mean and rude. If anything, it makes you not understand anything, but not like Down syndrome. You can understand, but you can't . . . make other people understand.

In this, Charlie tried to explain that his behavior was not always purposeful but could result from misunderstanding. He compared it to Down syndrome, perhaps to distinguish it as something closer to "normal." This is similar to how Cody described the teens in the group as different from people with autism who can't talk. This can make disability studies problematic in itself. Even the naming of them as disabilities merges them together in a category that some find troublesome. The hierarchies of power that are valued by society are often reflected even in the language of the marginalized.

AUTOBIOGRAPHY AS A COUNTERNARRATIVE

The works of the youth, those that directly took on the topic of autism and those that did not, all served to dismantle the frame of autism in some way. These autobiographies have the potential to change the conversation about autism. Troubling the ideology of normal is simply not enough to compensate for the practices embedded in society. Autobiographical works claiming disability for the author in a positive way builds an image of that author as capable of self-representation. This work is political in that it challenges the deeply ingrained social policies and practices surrounding individuals with disability (Campano & Simon, 2010). This work provides an alternative to the dominant medical model. As these autistic youth described themselves and their experiences, they offered a new perspective on autism.

One of the problems with the creation of counternarratives is that it is impossible from a practical standpoint to avoid the terms and meanings of the dominant discourse. But without counternarratives, we are pinned to the dominant stories as well. As counternarratives gain strength, the more dominant narratives begin to crack (hooks, 1989; Thomas, 1999). As bell hooks (1989) wrote, "Oppressed people resist by identifying themselves as subjects, by defining their reality, shaping their new identity, naming their history, telling their story" (p. 43). The students in our group, through telling their stories, *named* themselves and *resisted* an oppressive framework.

In a sense, the teens, in their formation of this group, highlighted their identification of themselves as autistic. They defined themselves as "other" as a natural part of fitting in with our group culture. However, to think of autism as culture necessitates setting them apart from the norm, othering them in a way that may increase marginalization to recognize culture. As Erickson (2010) describes:

> It should be noted, however, that an increase in the deliberateness and intensity of cultural awareness necessarily involves a comparative awareness. The construction of in-group identity is a relational process through which a definition of Other as well as of Self, of Them as well as of Us—and in the case of subordinated groups a specific identification of aspects of oppression—becomes more focal in conscious awareness. (pp. 43–44)

In this work, the youth had to describe themselves in terms of their differences, the ways in which they were unlike others. The work of othering themselves gave them greater agency to name their stories.

I am arguing here that these local accounts are a type of resistance. They demonstrate how the medical model is insufficient in describing these youth and their experiences. In fact, the stereotypes created by the positivist model are not only insufficient, but incomplete and incorrect. These are not individuals who are self-isolating or incapable of empathy. They are not people who lead *unautobiographical lives* (Smith, 1996). They have deep and rich emotional experiences and are accomplished in sharing those histories with others.

When asked what he would want others to know about autism, Cody responded, "I wish more people knew about autism generally. People don't understand it enough." These works are not merely self-expression. Because they speak back to the larger concepts of autism and disability, they are socially, culturally, and politically situated. The students responded intentionally to the misrepresentations that were made about them by others. Autobiography is of particular importance in this work because it can serve as a reevaluation of disability. The images and stories of the teens may not be entirely unique. They all share some common characteristics, and many of the youth shared common experiences of marginalization and oppression. It is their commonality to one another, and the common experiences they share with those *not* labeled autistic, that makes these stories unifying. As Carini (2001) explains, "The way of knowing something is irreducibly perspectival and value-imbued" (p. 78). Likewise, autism is more nuanced than any definition of it. We can only ever have a partial picture, as with knowing anything (Carini, 2001). The students' contributions to this picture through their works serve to construct autism in a more varied way. They counter the pathologizing of autism by centering their personal experiences. Throughout this chapter, I presented the youth's work to examine their own views of labeled identities. The students provided a strong counternarrative to the traditional understandings of autism. In the final chapter, I will discuss how these works are counter to the characterizations that are prevalent in the disability literature and explore the implications and promise of this kind of work.

CHAPTER 5

"I can do more than people think I can do"

On Discovering What We Seek

We see, in Chapter 1, some assumptions about autism that prevail in common understandings. As noted, Smith (1996) explains that the medicalized model relegates autistic people to an unautobiographical life. Additionally, Losh and Capps (2006) claim that people with autism lack emotional experiences deep enough to discuss. So, how did the work that the youth took up in this group counter these assumptions about autism? Billy's audio poetry was fraught with emotion. Cody's interactions showed a teen who was both connected and empathetic to others. Elizabeth's narratives pushed back against oppressive circumstances. Charlie's recordings examined his isolation, not of himself, but at the hands of his peers. All of the students, in ways both big and small, took up questions about their identities as autistic youth. They took risks in telling their stories and opened themselves up to one another and to the outside. They claimed their experiences as their own and crafted themselves as agents of their own narratives. And through all of this, they demonstrated deeply autobiographical lives.

In this chapter, I present several findings of this work and the evidence that informs them. I discuss these products and their significance to me, to the group, to the center, and to the larger community. I also present implications of this work that have the potential to inform policy, practice, and theory. Finally, I provide some suggestions for future research.

There are three overarching findings of this work:

1. The youth demonstrated an ability to create profound autobiographical works through which they located themselves and made personal connections.
2. As the students crafted their personal histories, the group became a space for inquiry in which the students were able to endure, resist, and reframe the oppressive experiences in their lives.
3. The teens' work is tied to the larger conversations about autism and serves as a counter-practice. Through the alternative

narratives that the teens constructed, they negotiated assumptions about autism and managed their own identities.

Each of these findings is discussed in detail in the three sections that follow.

AUTOBIOGRAPHICAL LIVES

The students, throughout the year and in a myriad of ways, engaged in the creation of autobiography. They located themselves in the work they created and demonstrated their autobiographical lives. This work was based on the idea that no life is unautobiographical. I believed that the teens would all tell their stories in different ways, but I always assumed they had stories to tell. This is also a basic premise on which the rest of the findings of this study are built. Freire (2000) wrote, "Those who have been denied their primordial right to speak their word must first reclaim this right and prevent the continuation of this dehumanizing aggression" (p. 88). Thus, I find it necessary to make this claim: that individuals with autism, like all other individuals, are able to and have a right to construct and express their life stories.

Through these autobiographical works, the teens positioned themselves as individuals capable of proficiencies that might be called into question by their labels of autism. One example is that the students made personal connections in and through their work; they demonstrated complex social understandings. Billy's audio poetry, for instance, shows deep and nuanced relationships to the members of his family. I also recognize this connectedness in Mark's photos of his father, in Elizabeth's text messages to her classmate, in Cody's videos of his sister, and in many other works.

The youth also held expectations of the world around them and reflected those expectations in their works. Billy felt that family should act a certain way; he made those expectations clear in his audio recordings and writing. Charlie and Mark were also explicit in their expectations of family. Others, like Carson, reflected on their expectations of not only family but peers as well. The teens demonstrated relief, disappointment, irritation, anxiety, and a host of other emotions in response to these expectations. They constructed images of responsibility, connectedness, and relationships throughout these autobiographical works.

In our group, we made room for the youth to represent themselves and their own experiences. These projects remind us not to limit the potential of students based on labels but to look beyond stereotypes to examine closely the valuable work that teens can do to describe themselves. These works challenge the notion that autistic people are unable to self-reflect. All of these teens were engaged in identity creation; they built portraits of themselves for an audience to view. They used some common media and shared language, but each project created a distinct portrait with individual ideals, values, and beliefs about the world. Generalizations about how individuals with autism make meaning can miss the nuanced abilities and realities that our students bring to the classroom and beyond.

CREATING FOR AGENCY

As the students crafted their personal histories, the Teen Project became a space for inquiry. I take up the same principles as Campano (2009), who explains that teachers conducting inquiry are:

> thus engaged in the infinitely complex and never-ending task of adjudicating between various categories and concepts, deciding which ones to provisionally accept . . . which ones to resist as damaging social distortions . . . which ones to push up against . . . and which ones to consider with a grain of salt. (p. 331)

I see my students as taking up these same tasks. Charlie used his work as a way to endure the aggression he faced and to legitimize his endurance. He decided to accept his position, perhaps tentatively, and explored that resolution in his work. Elizabeth, who time and again presented images of resistance, confronted her oppressive circumstances through this inquiry. She made choices about what work was worth undertaking in her life. Her claims of power, despite the often-negative consequences, allowed her to see herself as an agent in her own stories. And Cody, in his ever-complex representations of his experiences, made profound choices about how to represent himself. He created new narratives to replace those in which he was marginalized.

This was, as Carini (2001) names, a *collective work*, incorporating the voices of many authors. It took time, and responsiveness, and circularity. By this, I mean the group carefully returned, again and again, to the works they created, responding to one another and one another's works, creating and revising and creating anew with each circuit. It involved the gathering up of experiences and the making of new knowledge. Together, the students became a collaborative community, learning with and through one another's works. This happened when they all responded to Rachel's rap (Chapter 2), talked together with Elizabeth about school (Chapter 3), and constructed their own definitions of autism (Chapter 4). This work happened repeatedly and became embedded in the life of the group. This group provided a structure for the youth to gain agency. I saw this work done in all the ways they responded to how others viewed them and treated them. As previously noted, through this work, each teen began to "craft an agentive self" (Hull & Katz, 2006). For example, Elizabeth's work to assert herself as a young woman with strength was apparent in all her writing and drawing. Likewise, Cody's varying truths were a way for him to write himself as a powerful person, in control of his own stories.

AUTOBIOGRAPHY AS A COUNTER-PRACTICE

Not only is this an issue of how these students are labeled, but who does the labeling. When given the opportunity to represent themselves and their experiences, these youth offered a range of views on autism. As illustrated throughout the previous chapters, these views were sometimes outside the dominant lens, challenging the notions of autism as isolating and debilitating. In representing themselves, the teens constructed images of autism. They interrogated the social meaning of paradigms like *normal*. Through their work, the students managed their identities as people with autism and negotiated the assumptions that accompany such a label. Despite wrestling with issues of disclosure, the youth created rich and powerful and alternative narratives of autism.

In Charlie's exploration of autism, he attempted to position himself as *different but not wrong*. In Cody's definition, he questioned the entire paradigm of *normal*. Throughout these autobiographical works, the teens claimed themselves as experienced and enduringly capable. They resisted the stereotypes of the positivist model, situating themselves and their experiences as a response to the limiting assumptions of others.

I have argued here that the language of education, especially for those with disability, relies heavily on the negative—what they are not able to do, what skills need to be remediated, what gaps need to be filled. The language of education reform does not, as Carini (2001) notes, reflect a deep-rooted belief in children as *makers of knowledge*. Likewise, autobiographical accounts from individuals with disability are not often included in autism research (Kliewer & Biklen, 2001). The work the teens did is important because knowledge is always dependent upon its context: "It requires vigilance to keep before us the question of who benefits from a particular construction of knowledge, and who is ruled out by that construction" (Carini, 2001, p. 78). This work stands to unsettle the current constructions of autism. Charlie's definitions of autism, as well as Cody's and Elizabeth's explorations of normal and control, place the power of naming and defining back into the hands of those who are being labeled. This can be a powerful tool for them to own.

PRACTITIONER INQUIRY: MAKING MEANING FROM OUR WORK

When I began this work with the teens, I had some expectations of what I would find. Somehow, I had temporarily lost my way as a teacher committed to public education. I started to see school in opposition to the work the Teen Project was doing, despite my years in the classroom. I expected that I would find kids who were doing terribly in school, who had checked out from the educational process. I imagined their schools as unsupportive places where they were categorized and labeled and boxed in. I thought I would show this spectacularly rich work the students were producing in this after-school program as a contrast to the skill-and-drill work they were doing in school. Then I thought I might draw some conclusions about how multimedia work is engaging for them, say that this work should be done in schools, and wrap it all up with a nice clean bow. What I really found was messier, deeper, more complex, more nuanced, and I think, more profound.

I also expected that the literacies of all this would take center stage. I had hoped to show how these students could craft incredible works, producing more than they did in other spaces like school. I don't know why I was so determined to create this dichotomy of in-school/out-of-school literacies. When it came down to the actual works of the teens, I realized I had little evidence of what they were producing in school. I realized that some of the youth had wonderfully supportive school experiences and some did not. I realized that the really interesting activities that were happening in the group did not depend on the dichotomy that I had created in my imagination. I also began to approach all of their work as a demonstration of literacy. When I took up this stance, and I began to notice all of these threads woven intricately throughout the work, I could only see these teens as makers. It was no longer about what they *could do* in group and what they *did not do* in school. It grew and became more substantial, and more important. In retrospect, I realize I had been influenced by the negative discourse in which I was immersed. I also realized what an incredible hurdle this was to overcome. If someone like me, someone who was so aware of the dominant discourse and its oppressive effects, could become unmindful, what about everyone who is not even privy to this discussion?

What I think allowed me, as an individual, and us, as a group, to do this work was threefold:

1. I presumed that all of the youth in this group were capable of this intellectual work. This required a specific and deliberate mindset.
2. I spent a good deal of time and energy knowing these students personally and deeply. This required a commitment.
3. I valued greatly their work and their contributions. This was perhaps the most difficult. It was not until after I circled around

and back, time and time again, to this work that I started to see the value in every single piece.

Cochran-Smith and Lytle (2009) describe several main themes that weave throughout practitioner inquiry. The first of these, a commitment to exploring issues of equity, engagement, and agency, is an idea that has been prominent in my work. Part of this theme is the inclusion of students as participants in inquiry; teachers and students collaborate on the research, often with the aim of bringing about some change (Cochran-Smith & Lytle, 2009). Early in my career, I began questioning the ideas around authority and the possession of knowledge. I wrestled with, and continue to struggle with, thoughts around agency and representation. I consistently struggle between trying to represent my students in my work without positioning myself in authority over them, and I have found it very difficult to privilege their voices without overprivileging my own at the same time. It was important to my work to invite my students, the youth themselves, into this inquiry process. As a way of addressing my concerns about how privileged my voice could become, I invited my students to codesign the inquiry. Sometimes I recorded them, sometimes they recorded me, and very often they recorded one another. Sometimes I brought my stories, and sometimes they brought theirs. I was not always successful in this endeavor—often, when I'm replaying recordings of our group interactions or transcribing some of this work, I'm reminded of how dominant my own voice is. Of course, this is because of the fact that I was the leader of this inquiry, the teacher, the one who drove this kind of work in this space. It's a complicated dance, and one in which I was usually only fighting myself. I imagine that this group could have run without me or that the students didn't need my leadership to do this work, but it's not true. This is work about relationships, and even the youth themselves had issues around their own authority to tell their stories. So I led, creating a sort of curriculum and structure that I felt would benefit the group, our relationships, and their inquiry. I tried to question the notion of dominance as it pertained to the group and my leadership. Who I was in this group is an important part of this inquiry, and ultimately factors into the chapters that are written here.

This work was also highly dependent on my relationship with the youth in the group. Kliewer and Biklen (2001, 2007) refer to this as *local understanding*: "Local understanding of people with severe intellectual disabilities is born out of caring, interactive, and interdependent relationships in which both participants infer valued capacities and competence on the other" (2001, p. 4). In other words, this kind of work requires deep and understanding partnerships between teachers and students. This is not to imply that this work cannot be done in school and classrooms. In fact, teachers often know their students deeply and intimately enough to interpret their actions and intentions. What I am saying is that this research cannot be done in the absence of relationships or by casual observation. These are richer data with more profound uncoverings than we can find in "objective" testing.

We have to keep vigilant about this work, and about our stance. This is constantly present in our efforts at the center. It is work that *we did* and *are doing* and *will do*. It is work that places value on that making of knowledge that is not measured on progress reports or tested in examinations. We have to remind ourselves and our colleagues and our students to take up this serious work, and to do it in a way that is respectful of the places where everyone originates. We are so consumed by the everyday and by the many constraints that threaten this work. We are so inundated by the negative; it is in the many scores and reports we receive, the research articles we read, and the larger conversations in which we participate. This work was and is particularly challenging because of the positivist framework that is so dominant in the autism discourse. It takes focus and concentration to keep this work a priority.

This is the story of one teacher, just one teacher with a handful of students. This is also the story of a handful of students, just a handful of students with autism in an after-school program. This is the story of an after-school program, just an after-school program in an autism center in a small city. This is a story of a teacher and her students and an after-school program with ideas about what it meant to read and write and create to represent ourselves.

HOW WE MOVE FORWARD

Throughout this book, I have explained that limited understandings of autism can be countered by the real, autobiographical representations of autistic people themselves. These representations, however, need to be given voice. This section explores the possibilities for change in policy, research, and practice using this work and explorations like it.

Policy

During the writing of this book, I received two emails regarding former students, the messages arriving about a month apart. These two students were the first I had ever engaged in autobiographical exploration with; reflections on both of their autobiographies had become papers for my early doctoral work. The first email was from a friend who worked in city government; she told me that Jenny, a student I had taught in 3rd through 5th grades and whose work is discussed in Chapter 1, was interning at her office while attending art school. Jenny had struggled in her early elementary years to communicate and had attended a residential school for children with autism before coming to my class. She was buoyantly social and optimistic, engaging everyone she met.

Jenny loved making jewelry, drawing, and most of all, writing. She filled notebook after notebook in my class with her memories, her musings, and her dreams. She was my first student to blog and my first to keep a journal. She got in trouble in elementary school for talking too much and in high school for threatening to kiss the boys. I was thrilled to find that she had landed in such a great place. This email inspires me.

The other email was from a former student herself, Ellen. Ellen had great difficulty after leaving my classroom. This is not to imply that she did not have great difficulties during the 3 years I was her teacher; she certainly did. When she came to my classroom, she had already been removed from two other programs, one for breaking the teacher's arm. I have very vivid memories of meetings in which our staff struggled over her remaining in our class, if that was the right placement for her, if she belonged in public school, if we could keep Ellen and the other kids and the staff safe with her there. It's also not to imply that she didn't have great difficulties at home at the time, either. On several occasions, Ellen came to stay for the weekend at my house because her parents were urgently in need of a break. Now, at age 17, Ellen was in a long-term psychiatric facility halfway across the country. "It is good, not bad," she told me in the email, "because it will (I hope) fix some of my problem for now and forever." This email is devastating to me.

As educators, we have these incredible hopes that we can be the game-changers for our students. Maybe sometimes we are. Maybe sometimes we're not. It's a behemoth of a system to try to navigate. It's not just the institution of school that we're doing this work within—that in itself would be so much to tackle. It's the entire construction of autism and disability, the stigmatization, the medicalization, the marginalization, that makes this work so difficult. It's also what makes this work so important.

There are pervasive structures that limit people with autism. These structures are enacted daily in the practices of education and beyond. Kluth and Darmody-Latham (2003) point out that "students with autistic characteristics are too often dismissed from the literate community . . . excluded from rich and meaningful literacy experiences" (p. 533). All of the authors in Biklen's (2005) book except one were excluded from regular school experiences with peers. Autistic students are sometimes seen as unable to participate in literacy activities; other times, they are excluded to work on acquiring "life skills" (Kluth & Chandler-Olcott, 2008). Literacy policy and practice in schools can be de facto discrimination against students who have been historically devalued. As Delpit (1988) urges, we cannot "advocate a simplistic 'basic skills' approach for children outside the culture of power" (p. 24). It is our responsibility as leaders in the education community not only to make room for local knowledge but to make it a priority. This is not work that is ancillary or incidental to the real learning of schools. It is not even a necessary foundation for real learning to be done. This *is* the real learning that can be accomplished.

In today's educational climate of testing and standardization, the deficit view of students is more problematic than ever. We give test after test that measures one kind of learning in one kind of setting, leaving little room for the kinds of creative thinking some of our students do most brilliantly. This deficit view is especially apparent in special education. We write IEPs as though children are a sum of their strengths and needs, whittled down to a few paragraphs or bullet points. We create goals and objectives as though knowledge is a carrot pulled along on a string. It is so reductive. It is troublesome enough to create these documents of deficit, but their real purpose is to then guide teaching. Special education, in its quest to meet the individualized needs of each student, has been reduced to the inauthentic listing and teaching of discrete skills. This does not honor the real teaching and learning that can happen in our classrooms.

As discussed in the Preface, I began this work following what Biklen (2005) calls *the presumption of competence*, going in with the understanding that these youth were capable of this kind of exploration and representation. Taking this stance, I learned a great deal about competence from the teens themselves. Their knowledge and expertise were everywhere in this work, but I could have missed them if I were only looking for their deficits. This stance and this work make all the abilities of the students visible. I wish to extend this same *presumption of competence* to the teachers in their classrooms and out-of-school programs. What would we see if we assumed great work and looked for accomplishments? Teachers receive enough vilification from the school reformers and public commenters. We have to believe that classrooms can become a space for self-representation that respects the knowledge that these kids, and all kids, bring to school. We have to believe that school can become a place where our students feel safe and valued. We need schools to be a place that doesn't tear these students down but instead builds them up, making it possible for them to build knowledge together. As Carini (2001) explains:

> Until as educators and citizens we make room and time and educational arrangements that allow us to recognize, value, and draw forth this dimension of the children we educate, we will continue to be overwhelmed by their variety and diversity. We will continue to resort to categorizing them in order to reduce the complexity of the task. We will continue to seek technical, external solutions that will fix or alter the children so they will fit more easily into the school mold. (p. 171)

Our students come to us with an immense corpus of experiences. We, as educators, can choose to use that knowledge or we can be overwhelmed by it. Until we change our stance to one that honors the knowledge of our students, our teaching will continue to be undermined by the deficit perspective.

This was and is important work, not just as an academic exercise but as the laying of a foundation for this deliberate self-naming and self-describing and self-exploring for *all* autistic people. Those of us who are doing this kind of work need to take Carini's (2001) directives to task: to open this work up to others and one another, and to commit to supporting one another in this work in classrooms and beyond. This research can inform policy so that systems are set up to support more of this kind of work. The dominant discourse, the language of the media and the law and the medical community and the education reformers, continues to portray autism as a problem to be fixed (or at least accepted). In contrast, this work demonstrates that these students, and students like them in a variety of ways, are knowledgeable, talented, and capable.

Theory and Research

Throughout this work, I rethought my initial questions many times. I thought of a million other questions I could have asked instead or in addition, such as these:

- How did the youth form this inquiry group and what did it do for them?
- How did these students read and write and create for themselves, for others, for change?
- How did the teens craft themselves as agents in their own experiences?
- What purposes did all of this work serve?
- What issues did the youth agree and disagree on and how did they negotiate these issues?
- How could we appreciate the identities of these students in a new way?

I began to see Campano's (2007) question as my own:

> What would it mean to develop curricula that acknowledges our students' unique social identities, not as problems, but as profound sources of knowledge that could help us illuminate aspects of our shared world and inform the ways we conceptualize our pedagogies? (p. 16)

This is a far-reaching question, not limited to Campano's immigrant students but applicable to all classrooms. How can this speak to the frameworks of autism, disability, and education?

Autobiography holds a prominent place in critical disability studies. As Couser (2007) explains, autobiography is necessarily self-representative. As a result, it can serve as a counter to marginalization and push against the stigmas of disability. By controlling the story, disabled people can hold agency over how they are portrayed.

There are many autobiographical accounts from autistic people, with more being published each year. People like Temple Grandin (1986, 1995), Donna Williams (1992), and even Luke Jackson (2002, 2004) have been publishing their life experiences for years. The problem with these is that they are seen as anomalies, those few people with autism who have "broken free," at least long enough to communicate their ideas about autism (Bilken, 2005). What I am claiming is that the work we did in our Teen Project is *not* extraordinary. Given the space and supports, autistic people can create complex and compelling autobiographical accounts. Telling more of these stories, locally, individually, and repeatedly, is a way to push against this notion that autism is unautobiographical in most cases. The work done in our Teen Project needs to be done over and over again in a range of ways, in multiple spaces, and by a variety of people.

Practice

I was engaging my students in this kind of work before I knew what to call it, before I had been introduced to critical inquiry, before I had heard of disability studies. In the years since, I've come across many other teachers doing work like it, work in which they reject the stereotypes and standardization in favor of something they create with their students, something that honors the knowledge that kids like these bring to the classroom. I know there are many careful and driven educators who are doing this work under the radar from school reform every day. As Campano and Simon (2010) explain:

> thoughtful teachers have strong intuitive understandings of how the idea of the normal is a reductive, insufficient, and counter-productive way of understanding student potential. What is needed are specific and local accounts of how educators resist the normal curve to enact more democratic educational arrangements. (p. 222)

This work is one answer to that call. Much more of this kind of teaching is needed to resist the educational policies that push it down the list of priorities in favor of teaching discrete skills. More of this work is exactly what will give it value.

It may be helpful here as I am advocating for this work in practice to discuss some of the potential difficulties involved in engaging in this kind of teaching. I have also included a list of ideas to help an inquiry group get started (see Figure 5.1). I do think the use of technology, or at least the inclusion of it as one choice in the multiple modes available to the students, helped engage some of the teens in this work. In fact, several of the students cited their interest in technology as one of their reasons for joining the group. This really was not as simple as it sometimes seems throughout this book. Cameras and computers are certainly more expensive than paper and markers, for one thing. I had to make some hard choices and do extra work (like grant writing) to access the equipment we would need. We also used my own personal laptop to store, edit, and view all the photos, video, and digital audio. I had friends and family members who were willing to donate their old computers for this work. I realize that this may be prohibitively expensive for some classrooms and after-school programs that might not be able to access the same resources I could.

In the time since this particular group was engaged in this work, technology has become even more ubiquitous. Now, when I facilitate similar explorations with students, many of them have their own technology (like cellphones or tablets) that they use for pictures and videos. Many have social media accounts that they use regularly. I no longer have to supply equipment, but I always keep some options on hand for students who might not have the same access to technology as others.

I also want to make it clear that I am not, by any stretch of the imagination, a technology expert. In fact, the students often knew more than I did about the technical aspects of this work. In many cases, the technology added an extra layer of work for me. I also know that integrating technology into inquiry can be intimidating for some educators. I think I was realistic about what I could and could not do. I also was not expecting theater-quality finished projects. In fact, I was not expecting any finished

Figure 5.1. Ideas to Start an Inquiry Group

- Brainstorm a group list of ways to tell a story.
- Create individual lists of important life events and share with a partner.
- Pick a topic (friends, my life in school, things I find interesting) and take 10 photos.
- Video interview a family member about one of your accomplishments.
- Bring in artifacts of five things that are important to you.
- Draw a comic strip of a problem you have faced.
- Create a video tour of where you live or hang out.
- Take 10 selfies that show you as a student.
- Post to a social media page created for the group.
- Bring in five photos from when you were young and tell a story about each.
- Take photos of problems or issues you see and come up with action items as a group.

projects at all, in the traditional sense. I was interested in the *creating* more than the *creations*.

One hidden benefit to my lack of technological expertise was that it set up the teens as expert resources for one another. When one had trouble accessing a file or downloading from a camera, they went to one another for help instead of me. I think this helped even out the power relationship that was at play, even just a bit. It may not be necessary to teach these digital literacy skills in school, precisely because the youth themselves, from almost any background, are already more adept at their use than many teachers. Rather, these skills can be integrated tools for teaching and learning.

Also, I see clearly in this writing that the work was hard in that it was deep and complex and emotional. I think what may be hidden from view is that the facilitation of this work was difficult as well. Engaging, really and truly interacting with youth in a group on their terms, can be exhausting work. Understanding the needs and talents that such a diverse group of individuals brought with them each week was an enormous task. Some weeks it was difficult just to keep all of the equipment straight; other weeks it was hard to keep it from being broken. Once, a video camera was returned with a Post-it note stuck to it that read, "Waterlogged. Sorry." It was sometimes hard to keep the students on task, respectful of one another, and respectful of themselves and the work they were doing, all without fully taking over the group. I wanted them to have ownership over this group, this space, and this work. But sometimes I had to be more of an authority than I would have liked.

This work is also difficult to make space for in schools in light of the push to teach what is tested. As Campano (2007) explains:

> One, arguably dominant, response to this paradox is to compartmentalize diversity. We tend to agree that our differences should be "tolerated"—maybe even affirmed—but can the students read, have they acquired basic skills, and are their test scores rising? (p. 4)

This feels really present in my work. We do so much to fight bullying and to put teachers and classmates on the side of those who are marginalized. We promote diversity. But what we really do, beneath, above, and around all that talk about acceptance, is put labels on kids, and assign them numbers, groups, and goals and objectives. And we measure them. By law, we measure students with disability more than we measure any other student. We measure them again and again, and we report on these measurements, and we always list them as deficient in some way. We do it so they can qualify for services, so they can get certain accommodations, so they can be allowed some piece of flexibility that they might need. But we measure them and mark them as deficient, wrong, different, in order to get them this access. And does all that measuring even help? What would our students think if they saw these measurements? What would our students and their parents think if they instead saw measurements of what these students contribute?

I consider this work to be a form of what Kluth (2003) refers to as *subversive pedagogy*. It is teaching that rejects the current structures in favor of a more equitable practice. This subversive pedagogy can take many forms in our classrooms, from refusing a scripted curriculum to changing the language with which we write reports. It pushes against the systemic exclusion and oppression of marginalized students. In order to do this work, we must keep a critical lens on our teaching and the practices of our schools. It is all too easy to forget how important this work is when we are immersed in the culture and language of school reform. But we legitimize the oppressive practices by participating in them (Kluth, 2003). What we can do is take up an inquiry stance (Cochran-Smith & Lytle, 2009) in our classrooms every day. We can ask ourselves, "What would happen if I taught in a way that was more respectful of my students and their knowledge?" The purpose of this is social change from the bottom up. This work is meant to be disruptive.

MULTIMODALITY AND ACCESS

Although I do not see the use of technology as the point of this particular work, I do see this work as a useful contribution to works centering more on multimodality and technology. This work examines issues of identity for autistic adolescents through the use of multimodal literacies, including the autobiographical writings, art, video and audio productions, and photography of these adolescents. Heath and Street (2008) explain that the term *multimodal literacies* is used "to refer to those events and practices in which the written mode is still salient, yet embedded in other modes," which include modes to "transmit information, build skills, change attitudes, entertain, or accomplish all of these goals at the same time" (p. 22). These multimodal literacies include an expanded (and ever-expanding) view of texts. Text is not confined to writing or type on paper but can include other visual, auditory, and performative artifacts, including photography and video (Alvermann, 2007). Taking up a framework and understanding of literacy that utilizes digital media is not meant to exclude traditional reading and writing as "old" or "bad," but rather to supplement and expand what counts as literacy to engage new learners in the conversation, or to expand the communicative opportunities for those already engaged.

One subset of multimodal literacies is what Lundby (2008) and contributors call "Digital Storytelling," denoted as a specific form of media by the purposeful capital letters. This Digital Storytelling has three main characteristics:

1. It is small-scale in form (usually short clips).
2. It is small-scale in production (made with inexpensive and fairly accessible equipment and techniques).
3. It is small-scale in content (personal experiences in the first person).

Digital media can include audio, video, photography, blogging, mobile texting, social networking sites, and even tweeting; the boundaries of what counts as digital media are ever-expanding. In its essence, Digital Storytelling is a bottom-up practice; it is created at an individual level and does not require professional experience or any particular credentials. In this work, Digital Storytelling was not meant to obscure more traditional writing or nondigital art forms in this project but to provide additional outlets for expression (Hull & Nelson, 2005; Lundby, 2008).

The digital media that we utilized make up what Erstad and Wertsch (2008) term *new performance spaces*, and many users of certain digital media, like blogging, can find the relative anonymity very freeing. This may have particular relevance in works like those we created in the Teen Project, which are so deeply personal. Additionally, individuals sometimes struggle with face-to-face social relationships, and digital and online tools can be particularly useful. Through Facebook, I contacted an autistic friend, Elena, whom I know is very active in several online communities. When asked about this space for communication, she responded, "I woke up and started talking when I joined Facebook in January 2009. I am so much more comfortable talking with people online than in person, without those awkward pauses, and eye contact." Elena reports that she now has more than twice as many "online-only" friends than in-person friends, and that she communicates with them more often and in more depth than with those with whom she is friends offline. Digital media can create additional space for individuals to tell their stories.

Research on traditional notions of literacy and teaching has been increasingly infused with the use of technology. Bruce (2002), for example, emphasizes that "The new technologies thus challenge the educational system, but at the same time support an expanded view of learning, which welcomes change, responds to new media, and extends the classroom to connect with the larger society" (p. 3). In-school and out-of-school literacies can merge through the use of technology. Communication has changed drastically for today's youth, and many teens are regularly engaged digitally. Beach and Bruce (2002) argue that adolescent interactions with digital media allow identity construction alternative to the status quo. This has a potentially great impact on schools as places that must move from an understanding of information as a "limited commodity" to engage and develop their students (King & O'Brien, 2002). For some marginalized students, technology has given them unprecedented space for their voices to be heard.

Community(ies) is/are created, collapsed, and re-created. This can encourage inquiry in new and exciting ways.

I believe the use of technology in this work was not merely additive but transformative. The use of multiple modes was a constructive process in itself, and I think it changed the way the youth both saw and represented themselves. Some of the students, like Mark, found writing to be prohibitive to self-expression for a variety of reasons, including his struggle with fine motor skills. He found photography, however, to be a very fluid form of expression for himself. Others, like Elizabeth, simply refused to participate in anything they thought resembled schoolwork, which eliminated most pencil-and-paper tasks besides drawing. Many of the students found the inclusion of technology as a choice for expression to be empowering, even when they chose not to employ them. As Bruce (2002) explains, "Because it is an understanding, and not an inert artifact, the technology does not merely mediate changes in practices, but also catalyzes changes in social interaction, values, and power relations" (p. 15). The technology we used (or offered for use) in our group was more than just another selection in our expanded list of creative modalities. Instead, it created a new dynamic within which to work.

The multimodality of the teens' works was not the largest area of focus in this work. However, there are many aspects of this study left to be explored. I had to make choices to focus and dig deep into this project. Other choices, such as focusing on the multimodality of the work, might have yielded other interesting results. This could be one area for future study.

CONSIDERING MY OWN PLACE

Although I am not autistic, I am concurrently examining my own practice and the literacy practices of my students. My positionality as an outsider in collaboration with insiders (Herr & Anderson, 2005) is critical to this inquiry. I see this as the participatory method of colearning, which Herr and Anderson (2005) define as when "Local people and outsiders share their knowledge to create new understanding and work together to form action plans, with outsider facilitation" (p. 40). A major emphasis of this type of inquiry is access through relationships, and my relationship to the teens is of utmost importance. I have spent a great deal of time building relationships with my students, not for the purpose of this book but because I have spent years invested in this work and with these people about whom I care very much. I have also tried to build a group based on strong relationships, and I believe this model of cooperative inquiry adds to the validity of the study. As Herr and Anderson (2005) note, "For a study to have validity, authentic relationships must be maintained between group members and the initiating researchers as well as among group members themselves" (p. 45).

It is our responsibility as educators, researchers, and academics to question the ideology of normal. It is also our responsibility to push the locus of control away from the hegemonic traditions and toward the individuals themselves. This work makes the case that it is agentive for this group to name themselves. However, we cannot leave the bulk of responsibility for this power shift solely to the oppressed. We have a significant history of abuse, mistreatment, and isolation of the disabled in the United States. We cannot place the burden of such a leap on individuals with disability and expect them to have that kind of power. They may have the ability, but not always the power to do such work. It is our task to put the policies and practices in place to make room for this insider work. This work and the structures in which it must exist call for a joint effort between those with autism and those without.

Time and again, I just saw these teens as teens. Their diagnosis of autism is almost not present in some of these data. I did descriptive analyses (Himley, 2000, 2002) as I would for any student or child. I am placing, as Carini (2001) does, my "faith in an education centered on persons as ordinary" (p. 52). We need to ensure an education for *all* children that sees them as makers. It sends them the message that *everyone matters*. All children can do this work. It seems obvious in the context of this writing, but I feel the need to be specific: All students can do this work. This includes students with disability. This includes autistic students. This work is valuable.

This group was about creating space for students to represent themselves. Campano (2009) discusses the "humanizing" power of this self-representation, a model that provides students with "the freedom to participate in processes of educational self-determination and becoming" (p. 337). This notion of privileging student voices lays the groundwork for social activism in the questioning and repositioning of stereotypes. Campano's research, as with most practitioner inquiry, involves "valuing students' experiences as intellectual resources" (p. 333). With the dominant categorization and labeling of our students, their individual experiences and knowledge is often devalued. This work is an opportunity to foreground what these students know, live, sense, and can contribute. For students who have always been pathologized in their educational settings and beyond, creating space for self-representation can be an act of social justice (Campano, 2009; Cochran-Smith & Lytle, 2009).

As the education system pushes toward standardization, the complexity of our students and their individual differences are sometimes overlooked. Just as Carini (2001) does, this work also emphasizes the transformative power of assuming a humanizing stance and how that stance can expand possibilities in education. I center my work on a view of students as creators—creators of their stories and works about those stories. All people, including those labeled with disability, create meaning and their own understandings of the world. The purpose of this work is to value the knowledge of students and the contributions they bring to school.

This kind of work is not often done with autistic students. Even the creation of small pockets for this kind of learning to be taken up is important. This is work that *counts*. It matters for our students, and it matters for all students. We need to create spaces where we can work with autistic teens to endure hatred, resist oppression, and reframe the dialogue on autism. We need to create spaces for youth to form alliances, push one another, and hold one another up. We need to create spaces for them to represent themselves as agents for change.

Notes

Chapter 1

1. This gender division is very prominent at the center, with a large majority of males; it mirrors the overall rate of autism at a ratio of one female to every four males diagnosed. An exception to this is a "girls' group" at the center, which meets weekly to discuss issues of self-esteem with adolescent girls.

Chapter 2

1. Billy included some Spanish writing in these pieces, but he never explained why he did this. Spanish is not his home language; English and Russian are spoken in his home.

2. I still do not know what a "disky boy" is.

Chapter 3

1. For some of my students, equity is as fundamental as even having access to school. For example, Ivan had been placed on "homebound services;" his district felt it could not support Ivan's behavior needs and he was not allowed to attend school. Instead, the district provided a tutor at his home for 1 hour per day.

2. Many children with autism are provided with summer programs in their school districts, as mandated by special education law. For many of our students, this means attendance at a 6-week program, usually not in their regular school building and almost never with their regular schoolteacher. The intent of the law is to provide continuity of education to prevent regression, but for many of our students, the programming has become a time when they are isolated in almost empty buildings or bused to a central "special education" campus.

3. This may have been a fleeting friendship; Elizabeth never mentioned him again.

4. In Elizabeth's new class, she was the only girl.

Chapter 4

1. Although some members of the group rarely communicated verbally, none of the members of the teen program labeled themselves as "nonverbal." One group member was labeled as "nonverbal" in his school evaluation. He did speak at group, but his speech was sometimes difficult to understand. More than one group member used typing as his primary communication.

2. I am very aware here that there is no way for me to name the group of teenagers who do not have autism without engaging in the dominant discourse. Here, I use

the term *peers*, but a true peer group would not just be of the same age, but would also be of similar social status. Other terms, like *typical* or *normal*, are even more problematic in this kind of naming. Some in the autism community have created the term *neurotypical* to name those without autism, but even that term holds its own social value connotations.

References

Adichie, C. N. (2009, July). *The danger of a single story* [Video file]. New York, NY: TED Conferences. Retrieved from www.ted.com/talks/chimamanda_adichie _the_danger_of_a_single_story.html.

Alvermann, D. E. (2007). *Adolescents and literacies in a digital world.* New York, NY: Peter Lang.

American Psychiatric Association. (2013). *Diagnostic and statistical manual of mental disorders* (5th ed.). Washington, DC: Author.

Bakhtin, M. M. (1981). *The dialogic imagination: Four essays.* Carson, TX: University of Texas Press.

Barton, E. (2007). Disability narratives of the law: Narratives and counter-narratives. *Narrative, 15*(1), 95–112.

Barton, L. (1998). Sociology, disability studies, and education: Some observations. In T. Shakespeare (Ed.), *The disability reader: Social science perspectives* (pp. 53–64). New York, NY: Cassell.

Bauman, R., & Briggs, C.L. (1990). Poetics and performance as critical perspectives on language and social life. *Annual Review of Anthropology, 19*, 59–88.

Beach, R., & Bruce, B. (2002). Using digital tools to foster critical inquiry. In D. E. Alvermann (Ed.), *Adolescents and literacies in a digital world* (pp. 147–163). New York, NY: Peter Lang.

Biklen, D. (2005). *Autism and the myth of the person alone.* New York, NY: New York University Press.

Blackburn, M. V. (2002). Disrupting the (hetero)normative: Exploring literacy performances and identity work with queer youth. *Journal of Adolescent & Adult Literacy, 46*(4), 312–324.

Blackburn, M. V. (2003). Exploring literacy performances and power dynamics at the loft: "Queer youth reading the world and the word." *Research in the Teaching of English, 37*(4), 467–490.

Blackburn, M. V. (2005). Agency in borderland discourses: Examining language use in a community center with black queer youth. *Teachers College Record, 107*(1), 89–113.

Blackman, L. (2001). *Lucy's story: Autism and other adventures.* London, England: Jessica Kingsley.

Bruce, B. (2002). Diversity and critical social engagement: How changing technologies enable new modes of literacy in changing circumstances. In D. E. Alvermann (Ed.), *Adolescents and literacies in a digital world* (pp. 1–18). New York, NY: Peter Lang.

Campano, G. (2007). *Immigrant students and literacy: Reading, writing, and re-membering.* New York, NY: Teachers College Press.

Campano, G. (2009). Teacher research as a collective struggle for humanization. In M. Cochran-Smith & S. Lytle (Eds.), *Inquiry as stance: Practitioner research for the next generation* (pp. 326–341). New York, NY: Teachers College Press.

Campano, G., & Simon, R. (2010). Practitioner research as resistance to the "normal curve." In C. Dudley-Marling & A. Gurn (Eds.), *The myth of the normal curve* (pp. 221–240). New York, NY: Peter Lang.

Carini, P. F. (2001). *Starting strong: A different look at children, schools, and standards.* New York, NY: Teachers College Press.

Centers for Disease Control and Prevention (CDC). (2018). Data & statistics on autism spectrum disorder. Retrieved from www.cdc.gov/ncbddd/autism/data.html

Cochran-Smith, M., & Lytle, S. (2009). *Inquiry as stance: Practitioner research for the next generation.* New York, NY: Teachers College Press.

Cole, A. L., & Knowles, J. G. (2001). *Lives in context: The art of life history research.* Walnut Creek, CA: AltaMira Press.

Couser, G. (2007). Undoing hardship: Life writing and disability law. *Narrative, 15*(1), 71–84.

Delpit, L. (1988). The silenced dialogue: Power and pedagogy in educating other people's children. *Harvard Educational Review, 58*(3), 280.

Devlin, R., & Pothier, D. (2006). Introduction: Toward a critical theory of dis-citizenship. In D. Pothier & R. Devlin (Eds.), *Critical disability theory: Essays in philosophy, politics, policy, and law* (pp. 1–24). Vancouver, BC: UBC Press.

Engel, D., & Munger, F. (2007). Narrative, disability, and identity. *Narrative, 15*(1), 85–94.

Erickson, F. (2010). Culture and society in educational practices. In J. Banks & C. A. McGee Banks (Eds.), *Multicultural education: Issues and perspectives.* Hoboken, NJ: John Wiley.

Erstad, O., & Silseth, K. (2008). Agency in digital storytelling: Challenging the educational context. In K. Lundby (Ed.), *Digital storytelling, mediatized stories: Self-representations in new media* (pp. 213–232). New York, NY: Peter Lang.

Erstad, O., & Wertsch, J. V. (2008). Tales of mediation: Narrative and digital media as cultural tools. In K. Lundby (Ed.), *Digital storytelling, mediatized stories: Self-representations in new media* (pp. 21–40). New York, NY: Peter Lang.

Finkelstein, V. (1998). Emancipating disability studies. In T. Shakespeare (Ed.), *The disability reader: Social science perspectives* (pp. 28–52). New York, NY: Cassell.

Franits, L. (2005). The issue is—nothing about us without us: Searching for the narrative of disability. *American Journal of Occupational Therapy, 59,* 577–579.

Freire, P. (2000). *Pedagogy of the oppressed.* New York, NY: Continuum.

Gallagher, S. (2004). Understanding interpersonal problems in autism: Interaction theory as an alternative to theory of mind. *Philosophy, Psychiatry, and Psychology, 11*(3), 199–217.

Gee, J. (1996). *Social linguistics and literacies: Ideology in discourses* (2nd ed.). London, England: Taylor & Francis.

Gee, J. (2000). The new literacy studies: From "socially situated" to the work of the social. In D. Barton, M. Hamilton, & R. Ivanic (Eds.), *Situated literacies: Reading and writing in context* (pp. 180–196). New York, NY: Routledge.

Gill, M. (2004). Disability counter-narrative: Transforming ideas among high school students. *Disability Studies Quarterly*, 24(4). Retrieved from dsq-sds.org/article /view/879/1054

Goodman, S. (2003). *Teaching youth media: A critical guide to literacy, video production, and social change.* New York, NY: Teachers College Press.

Grandin, T. (1995). *Thinking in pictures: And other reports from my life with autism.* New York, NY: Doubleday.

Grandin, T., & Scariano, M. M. (1986). *Emergence: Labeled autistic.* Novato, CA: Arena Press.

Grotevant, H. D., & Cooper, C. R. (1998). Individuality and connectedness in adolescent development: Review and prospects for research on identity, relationships, and context. In E. E. Aspaas Skoe & A. L. von der Lippe (Eds.), *Personality development in adolescence: A cross-national perspective* (pp. 3–37). London, England: Routledge.

Heath, S. B., & Street, B. (2008). *On ethnography: Approaches to language and literacy research.* New York, NY: Teachers College Press.

Herr, K., & Anderson, G. (2005). *The action research dissertation: A guide for students and faculty.* Thousand Oaks, CA: Sage.

Himley, M. (with Carini, P. F.). (2000). *From another angle: Children's strengths and school standards: The Prospect Center's descriptive review of the child.* New York, NY: Teachers College Press.

Himley, M. (2002). *Prospect's descriptive processes: The child, the art of teaching, & the classroom & school.* North Bennington, VT: The Prospect Center.

Holland, D., & Lachicotte, W., Jr. (2007). Vygotsky, Mead, and the new sociocultural studies of identity. In H. Daniels, M. Cole, & J. V. Wertsch (Eds.), *The Cambridge companion to Vygotsky* (pp. 101–135). Cambridge, England: Cambridge University Press.

hooks, bell. (1989). *Talking back: Thinking feminist, thinking black.* Boston, MA: South End Press.

Hull, G. (2003). At last: Youth culture and digital media: New literacies for new times. *Research in the Teaching of English*, 38(2), 229–233.

Hull, G., & Katz, M. (2006). Crafting an agentive self: Case studies of digital storytelling. *Research in Teaching English*, 41(1), 43–81.

Hull, G., & Nelson, M. E. (2005). Locating the semiotic power of multimodality. *Written Communication*, 22(2), 224–261.

Individuals with Disabilities Education Act of 2004, 20 U.S.C.A. § 1400.

Jackson, L. (2002). *Freaks, geeks, and Asperger syndrome: A user guide to adolescence.* London, England: Jessica Kingsley.

Jackson, L. (2004). Luke's story. In H. Molly & L. Vasil (Eds.), *Asperger syndrome, adolescence, and identity: Looking beyond the label.* London, England: Jessica Kingsley.

Kaare, B. H., & Lundby, K. (2008). Mediatized lives: Autobiography and assumed authenticity in digital storytelling. In K. Lundby (Ed.), *Digital storytelling, mediatized stories: Self-representations in new media* (pp. 105–122). New York, NY: Peter Lang.

King, J. R., & O'Brien, D. G. (2002). Adolescents' multiliteracies and their teachers' needs to know: Toward a digital détente. In D. E. Alvermann (Ed.), *Adolescents and literacies in a digital world* (pp. 40–50). New York, NY: Peter Lang.

Klein, F. (2001). Retrieved from web.archive.org/web/20080210113402rn_1/home.
att.net/~ascaris1/

Kliewer, C., & Biklen, D. (2001). School's not really a place for reading: A research
synthesis of the literate lives of students with severe disabilities. *Research and
Practice for Persons with Severe Disabilities, 26*(1), 1–12.

Kliewer, C., & Biklen, D. (2007). Enacting literacy: Local understanding, significant
disability, and a new frame for educational opportunity. *Teachers College Record, 109*(12), 2579–2600.

Kluth, P. (2003). *"You're going to love this kid!" Teaching students with autism in
the inclusive classroom.* Baltimore, MD: Brookes.

Kluth, P., & Chandler-Olcott, K. (2008). *"A land we can share": Teaching literacy
to students with autism.* Baltimore, MD: Brookes.

Kluth, P., & Darmody-Latham, J. (2003). Beyond sight words: Literacy opportunities for students with autism. *The Reading Teacher, 56*, 532–535.

Lesko, N. (1996). De-naturalizing adolescence: The politics of contemporary representations. *Youth and Society, 28*(2), 139–161.

Lesko, N. (2012). *Act your age! A cultural construction of adolescence* (2nd ed.).
New York, NY: Taylor & Francis.

Losh, M., & Capps, L. (2006). Understanding of emotional experience in autism:
Insights from the personal accounts of high-functioning children with autism.
Developmental Psychology, 42(5), 809–818.

Lundby, K. (Ed.). (2008). *Digital storytelling, mediatized stories: Self-representations in new media.* New York, NY: Peter Lang.

McLean, K., Breen, A., & Fournier, M. (2010). Constructing the self in early, middle, and late adolescent boys: Narrative identity, individuation, and well-being.
Journal of Research on Adolescence, 20(1), 166–187.

Molloy, H., & Vasil, L. (2004). *Asperger syndrome, adolescence, and identity:
Looking beyond the label.* London, England: Jessica Kingsley.

Pahl, K., & Rowsell, J. (2006). *Travel notes from the new literacy studies: Instances
of practice.* Tonawanda, NY: Multilingual Matters.

Peters, S. (1999). Transforming disability identity through critical literacy and the
culture of politics of language. In M. Corker & S. French (Eds.), *Disability discourse* (pp. 103–115). Philadelphia, PA: Open University Press.

Phelan, P., Davidson, A. L., & Yu, H. C. (1998). *Adolescent worlds: Negotiating
family, peers, and school.* New York, NY: Teachers College Press.

Priestly, M. (1999). Discourse and identity: Disabled children in mainstream high
schools. In M. Corker & S. French (Eds.), *Disability discourse* (pp. 92–102).
Philadelphia, PA: Open University Press.

Riessman, C. K. (1993). *Narrative analysis.* Newbury Park, CA: Sage.

Riessman, C. K. (2008). *Narrative methods for the human sciences.* Thousand
Oaks, CA: Sage.

Rimland, B. (1986). Foreword. In T. Grandin & M. M. Scariano, *Emergence: Labeled autistic* (pp. 1–4). Novalo, CA: Arena Press.

Rimland, B. (1992). Foreword. In D. Williams, *Nobody nowhere: The extraordinary
autobiography of an autistic* (pp. ix–xii). New York, NY: Avon.

Shore, S. (2004). *Ask and tell: Self-advocacy and disclosure for people on the autism
spectrum.* Shawnee Mission, KS: Autism Asperger Publishing.

Singer, J. (1999). "Why can't you be normal for once in your life?" From a "problem with no name" to the emergence of a new category of difference. In M. Corker & S. French (Eds.), *Disability discourse* (pp. 59–67). Philadelphia, PA: Open University Press.

Smith, S. (1996). Taking it to the limit one more time: Autobiography and autism. In S. Smith & J. Watson (Eds.), *Getting a life: Everyday uses of autobiography* (pp. 226–246). Minneapolis, MN: University of Minnesota Press.

Thomas, C. (1999). Narrative identity and the disabled self. In M. Corker & S. French (Eds.), *Disability discourse* (pp. 47–56). Philadelphia, PA: Open University Press.

Waltz, G. (Producer), & Pentzell, N. (Director). (2002). *Outside/inside* [Motion picture]. United States: Sprout Films.

Wenger, E. (1999). *Communities of practice: Learning, meaning, and identity*. London, England: Cambridge University Press.

Williams, D. (1992). *Nobody nowhere: The extraordinary autobiography of an autistic*. New York, NY: Avon.

Williams, D. (2015). *Somebody somewhere: Breaking free from the world of autism*. New York, NY: Broadway Books.

Wilson, J. C., & Lewiecki-Wilson, C. (2001). *Embodied rhetorics: Disability in language and culture*. Carbondale, IL: Southern Illinois University Press.

Young, J. P., Dillon, D. R., & Moje, E. B. (2002). Shape-shifting portfolios: Millennial youth, literacies, and the game of life. In D. E. Alvermann (Ed.), *Adolescent literacies in a digital world* (pp. 114–131). New York, NY: Peter Lang.

Index

The letter *f* or *n* following a page number refers to a figure or note, respectively.

About the Author

Dr. Beth A. Myers is the Lawrence B. Taishoff Assistant Professor of Inclusive Education and executive director of the Taishoff Center for Inclusive Higher Education at Syracuse University. She oversees InclusiveU, a federally recognized model program for college students with intellectual and developmental disabilities. After teaching in an inclusive elementary autistic support program, Beth Myers opened a regional center for autism services in 2006 and served as executive director before joining the center's consultation team in 2011. She has provided school consultations and staff development to over 70 school districts. Myers serves on the National Down Syndrome Society Inclusion Committee and is the founding executive co-editor of the *Journal of Inclusive Postsecondary Education*. Beth lives with her husband and four children in Syracuse, New York.